TRAIN COUNTRY

Other Books by Donald MacKay

The Lumberjacks 1978

Anticosti: The Untamed Island 1979

Scotland Farewell: The People of the Hector 1980

Empire of Wood: The MacMillan Bloedel Story 1982

Heritage Lost: The Crisis in Canada's Forests 1985

The Asian Dream: The Pacific Rim and Canada's National Railway 1986

The Square Mile: Merchant Princes of Montreal 1987

Flight from Famine: The Coming of the Irish to Canada 1990

The People's Railway: A History of Canadian National 1992

TRAIN COUNTRY

AN ILLUSTRATED HISTORY OF
CANADIAN NATIONAL RAILWAYS

Donald MacKay & Lorne Perry

Douglas & McIntyre

Vancouver / Toronto

Douglas & McIntyre
1615 Venables Street
Vancouver, British Columbia
V5L 2H1

Canadian Cataloguing in Publication Data
MacKay, Donald, 1925—
Train country

ISBN 1-55054-441-1

1. Canadian National Railways—History. 2. Railroads—
Canada—History—20th century. I. Title

HE2810.C14M322 1994   385'.06'571   C94-910138-9

Editing and design by Robin Brass
Cover Design by Roberto Dosil (Praxis Design) and Peter Cocking
Cover photographs courtesy CN Photo Library
Printed and bound in Canada by Friesens
Printed on acid-free paper ∞

CONTENTS

PREFACE

No NATION OWES MORE TO THE STEEL WHEEL ON THE STEEL RAIL, THOUGH IT IS not always clear whether railways were built to unite Canada or Canada was created to justify railway-building. Building railways was such a lucrative and popular enterprise that there were nearly a score of them in British North America when Canada was born in 1867 – amid promises that more would soon be built to bond east and west.

In the event, the Intercolonial Railway between Halifax and Quebec was financed in the 1870s by the federal government, which also backed the Canadian Pacific Railway to Vancouver ten years later. Politically, economically and socially the railways that had begun to spring up under the generous encouragement of the Railway Guarantee Act of 1849 held the inside track of Canadian history for a hundred years. In the past thirty-five years, however, the railway industry has changed more profoundly than most.

As railways cut costs and staff and generally rationalize their resources and gear up for the twenty-first century, *Train Country*, a nostalgic photographic companion to *The People's Railway: A History of Canadian National*, published in 1992, recalls the people and machines that made Canada's biggest railway, and once its biggest business, so much a part of Canadian life.

Though Canadian National, as such, is little more than seventy years old, you will find many images of earlier vintage because CN is a paradox – at once the youngest and the eldest of Canada's railways. Many of the companies that

Some of the finest steam train photographs were made after regular operations had ceased in 1960. Northern type No. 6218 was probably the most photographed locomotive on CN's roster, and this close-up of its steam-shrouded driving wheels captures the power of these giants of the rails. Maintained in immaculate condition, it operated on dozens of excursions by railway enthusiasts in the late 1960s. (J. Norman Lowe photo)

7

went into the formation of CN in the five years after World War I date from the nineteenth century, and some very early in the century at that, like the pioneer Champlain and St. Lawrence Railroad Company, which began operations in 1836. The Grand Trunk and the Great Western, already major railways thirty years before the Grand Trunk declined government pressure to build to the West Coast and gave the task to the Canadian Pacific, were responsible for half a dozen Canadian "firsts," including sleeping, dining, parlour and mail-sorting cars and the first locomotive designed to burn coal rather than wood. In the late 1920s CN itself pioneered one of North America's first main-line diesels.

In a book of this size and nature it has been impossible to detail the infinite variety of a century and a half of rail operations through many regions with varying needs and conditions. Though the book includes the progress of technology, as well as the romance of yesteryear, it generally travels the main line.

Since it is hard to imagine nineteenth-century machinery on which more ingenuity was lavished, you will find a wide range of the "tea kettles and the dinosaurs" that most vividly recall the age of steam. A steam locomotive, from its air pump down through the alphabet to its turret pipe, had close to four hundred separate parts and, unlike the mass-produced diesel that replaced it, each steamer was more or less unique. As the engineers who drove them, gave them pet names and polished them daily would have told you.

Such was their quest for speed and economy that advances in train technology threatened to outstrip the communications vital to safety. To avoid confusion and calamity, they relied on two instruments in particular: the telegraph and the "railway deity," the railway pocket watch that was carefully synchronized among train crew and dispatcher at the start of every journey.

Most of the photographs, selected and researched by Lorne Perry, retired after forty years in the Public Affairs and Advertising department, are from the CN Photo Library. All but a few are published in book form for the first time.

While the authors are responsible for errors and omissions in the final product, we have not laboured alone. We thank J. Norman Lowe of Brockville, Ontario, CN's History Officer Emeritus, who kindly read early stages of the manuscript, as did J.L. "Jack" Cann of Toronto, former Vice-president of Operations. Broadcaster Bill McNeil of Toronto and Ken Mackenzie of Saltspring Island, British Columbia, the former CN archivist, who did so much to get CN's history project on the rails, provided many of the interviews that went into the book. Jean B. Héguy and Debbie Laramee of Montreal, and John MacRae of Elmsdale, Nova Scotia, provided additional photos.

We are grateful for the interest of Brant Ducey, retired CN Vice-president of Public Affairs and Advertising, Roger Cameron of Public Affairs, Connie Romani and the staff of the CN Photo Library, and Fiona Murray, Carol Patterson and the staff of the CN Library. Finally, our thanks to editor/designer Robin Brass of Toronto for putting it all together and to publisher Scott McIntyre for embracing the project so wholeheartedly.

DONALD MacKAY
Montreal, 1994

A NOTE ABOUT THE PICTURES
All photographs are from the CN Photo Library except where otherwise credited. The diagrams were drawn by Lorne Perry.

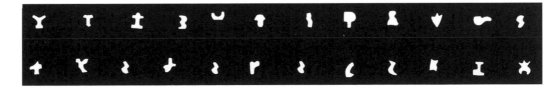

Each passenger train conductor had a ticket punch with a distinctive cut, which permitted auditors to verify ticket collection practices. Every ticket was cancelled by punching, once to indicate it could be used for further stages of the same journey, twice to indicate completion of the journey. The *click-click* sound as the conductor came into a coach was usually enough to cause regular travellers to dig out their tickets.

Conceived as a "farmers' railway" in western Canada, the Canadian Northern, one of the principal predecessors of Canadian National Railways, relied on fine old workhorses like this Ten Wheeler. Built by Brooks in the United States in 1902, No. 1261 was absorbed into CN when the Canadian Northern failed and it continued in service until 1945. (Ontario Archives)

1

TEA KETTLES
AND DINOSAURS

A WHOLE GENERATION HAS MISSED THE PLEASURES OF A STEAM TRAIN whistling across the country under a white mane of smoke. The drama of fiery monsters rumbling through Main Street, the luxury of plush and mahogany hotels on wheels, the elegance of four-course meals, crested silver and china, live only in the memories of people of a certain age. Noble beaux arts railway stations echo now to the twice-daily scurry of commuters or have been supplanted by undistinguished little buildings perched on the edge of town.

Thirty years have passed since the mighty steam locomotive, born in the Industrial Revolution and killed by the internal combustion engine, faded into museums to join the bones of dinosaurs. But it is worth recalling that for 120 years the steam locomotive, with its six-foot driving wheels, keening whistle, and aroma of hot steam, warm oil and acrid coal smoke, was king of transportation – the symbol of national prosperity and an integral part of our lives.

A concomitant of Confederation, key to commercial farming, backbone of commerce, and the making of small-town Canada, the railway linked farm to market, forest to factory, and mine to mill. For the first time in history people could travel a sizable distance in comfort. What had taken weeks with horse and wagon took days on a train; almost anyone who travelled more than ten or twenty miles left the horse in the pasture.

The railway encouraged business travel, produced the ubiquitous travelling salesman, fetched your new clothes, medicine, mail and telegrams, and carried your produce. "You'd see people coming up with their horses and sleighs to bring in their cream and butter and stuff," recalled locomotive engineer Graham Crossman of Saskatoon. "When you went through small towns whistling at night, they would flick their lights. Sometimes you'd even get a postcard from them. They liked it when you blew the whistle or waved. I miss that part of it. That's part of history now."

No country had greater need for transcontinental transportation, but against such forbidding terrain as the Canadian Shield and the Rockies, the "tea kettles"

The wood-burning *Prince of Wales* carried the future King Edward VII from Saint John to Rothesay, New Brunswick, in 1860. The coach was built for his visit by the European and North American Railway, later assimilated into the Intercolonial.

built in the 1830s in England for a tamer landscape were little more than toys. The thirteen-foot, wood-burning *Dorchester*, or Kitten as it was fondly called, had no cab and pulled two gaily painted wooden coaches. Six years after George Stephenson's famous *Rocket* had demonstrated in England that the steam locomotive was here to stay, the *Dorchester* was put into service in July 1836 by the Company of Proprietors of the Champlain and St. Lawrence Railroad. The 127th locomotive built by Robert Stephenson and Company of Newcastle, England, it puffed along at fifteen miles an hour over wooden rails topped with metal straps, some fifteen miles from Laprairie Wharf, facing Montreal across the St. Lawrence River, to St. Jean, Quebec, on the Richelieu River, where passengers transferred to vessels plying Lake Champlain and the Hudson River to New York.

By 1850, when the United States had more than nine thousand miles of rail, Canada possessed less than a hundred. But due to the Railway Guarantee Act of 1849, which encouraged private capital by guaranteeing interest on investment, trackage increased tenfold in a very few years. The new lines included the Grand Trunk Railway and the Great Western Railway, which between them served southern Quebec and Ontario.

In 1856 the Grand Trunk linked Montreal to Toronto. When travellers stepped aboard the train, carpetbag in hand, they were riding in the dawn of

intercity steam travel. In fact, had they tried to make the trip earlier than October 27 that year, it is doubtful they could have made it in one go as the Grand Trunk had been completed in sections. The first through train was an exciting occasion. Long before the train pulled out of Montreal a great crowd gathered to shout *bon voyage* and the greeting at Toronto was scarcely less hearty.

The Grand Trunk's wood-burning engines, perfuming the right-of-way with the smoke of beech and maple, were strong enough to haul seven coaches at thirty miles an hour, though the trip between Montreal and Toronto took seventeen hours. The decorative little No. 39 passenger engine, built in Birkenhead, England, stopped frequently for four-foot lengths of cordwood and to scoop up water from streams so the boiler would not blow up. It was so light that it was often crippled in winter by ice and snow, which could strand a train far out in the countryside.

A snowplow train pauses at St. Agapit, Quebec, on the Grand Trunk line connecting Lévis and the line between Montreal and Portland at Richmond, Quebec. The locomotive is a 4-4-0 American type, a wood-burner with a diamond stack. The plow is constructed largely of wood. (Metropolitan Toronto Reference Library)

To save forests along the right-of-way from catching fire, smokestacks with primitive spark arresters appeared in the shape of cabbages, mushrooms and diamonds. Cast-iron wheels increased safety. Enclosed cabs protected crews from weather and smoke. Like ships, engines had names, such as the Great Western's *Adam Brown* and the pioneer coal-burner *Samson*, which had worked the coal mines in Pictou County, Nova Scotia, since 1839. The elegant *Josephine* in Ontario was the fastest passenger engine of her time, though reports she once reached sixty miles an hour may have been exaggerated.

In Hamilton the Great Western built an opulent sleeping car in 1857, said to be a model for George Pullman's famous cars produced in Chicago two years later. Running between Niagara Falls and Detroit, it had three tiers of berths, heavy green curtains on the aisles, and spring beds with hair mattresses, quilts and feather pillows. Oil lamps had replaced paraffin candles, but coal stoves were still a menace in a swaying carriage full of sleeping people. The Great Western also built a "hotel coach," the first diner, so that passengers no longer had to snatch hurried meals at station stops.

Every station had a semaphore order board. The arms, one for each direction, are set here to the clear position, meaning there are no train orders to pick up.

In 1860 there were 2,138 miles of track in Canada, compared with 31,000 in the United States. In its search for speed, power and stability, the Grand Trunk had adopted the rugged, dual-purpose "American type" locomotive, which was to serve Canadian railways for more than a generation. Popular in passenger service, it also could haul a freight train at twenty-five miles an hour and its 4-4-0 wheel configuration meant it had four driving wheels plus four wheels on the leading truck to guide the engine around curves.

The Grand Trunk had 206 locomotives in 1860 and its shops at Point St. Charles, Montreal, where rolling stock was repaired and built, became a city of steam covering thirty acres, with foundries, rolling mills and 2,500 boilermakers, machinists, electricians, pipefitters, carpenters, moulders and other artisans. The first engine built there was the *Trevithick* to pull the royal train of the Prince of Wales, later King Edward VII, in 1860. Though only thirty-three tons, it was the giant of its day. For the occasion, the Grand Trunk built Canada's first fancy parlour car, with air conditioning provided by blocks of ice.

The highlight of the prince's visit was the opening of Montreal's Victoria Bridge (also built by Robert Stephenson), which the prince said was "unsurpassed by the grandeur of Egypt or Rome." Its tubular spans, supported by piers of lime-

Fifty Grand Trunk Railway locomotives were built at the Canada Works, Birkenhead, England, in the 1850s for North American terrain and climate. The Birkenhead here was purchased from the GTR by the little Carillon and Grenville Railway, which later became a small part of CN between Montreal and Ottawa.

Carved wood, gilding and tufted velour. Despite the Victorian splendour of the Grand Trunk Railway sleeping car, gaslights were dim and horsehair mattresses lumpy, and soot blew in the windows in the absence of air conditioning.

stone, arched across the St. Lawrence River to assure Montreal's primacy as the country's commercial capital for another hundred years.

In the same year the Great Western built the first main-line Canadian locomotive to burn coal. Though coal was more efficient and spark-free than wood, engine crews had to give up their traditional efforts to keep cabs spotless. When coal appeared in the tenders, engineers traded their gentlemanly "biled" shirts and top hats and became blue-collar workers in caps, overalls and bandanas.

In the beginning, railways were so small a train had the track to itself. But when two trains began to share a single track, timing became vital and passing sidings had to be added, along with semaphores that pointed upward for safety

When dining cars appeared, nineteenth-century trains no longer had to halt at station restaurants at mealtime. But tasselled window curtains, gaslights and condiments on shelves between the windows went out with the Victorians.

and downward for danger. When the telegraph appeared in the late 1840s, it became an essential tool of railroading. Operators were posted in stations across the country to provide surveillance and transmit orders from dispatchers to train crews about how and when to proceed.

Couplings consisted of an iron bar with a hole in each end and iron pins stuck into the holes. Though better than the original system of chaining cars together, manually operated link-and-pin couplers were dangerous to life and limb, for a brakeman had to step between the cars to guide the metal link into the drawbar and drop in the pin. When automatic couplers came into use, the impact of two cars meeting was sufficient to couple them without a brakeman having to intervene.

"I have to smile as I recall the trains that used to run out of Toronto in the old days," said D. J. McMillan, who became a railroader in 1876 and retired as a CN divisional superintendent in 1928, the year before the new 326-ton Northern type locomotives hauled passenger trains faster than a mile a minute.

"In those days our average train ran about fifteen cars, whose capacity was about ten tons a car. In the early days of railroading, coal-burning locomotives were a thing of the future. We used to burn cordwood and had 'wooding up' stations with hundreds of cords. Each tender held one cord of eighteen-inch wood. There was great rivalry between the engineers as to which one could operate his engine at least cost to the company. Many an engineer I have seen cursing his luck because his engine was seriously heavy on fuel, and I have often seen a train at a standstill and unattended on the line while the crew, like small boys hooking apples, climbed over the fence to raid some farmer's woodpile.

"Travel in the early days was more or less of a gamble. We had no snow-fighting equipment, other than shovels and the strong backs of the male passengers and crew. When the trains got stalled in a snowdrift, out would come the snow

Railway companies built the stoutest bridges on the continent. A dozen wood-burning locomotives, weighing a total of 854 tons, were assembled to demonstrate the strength of the New Hartford Bridge built in 1887 on the Central Vermont Railway, which later became a part of CN.

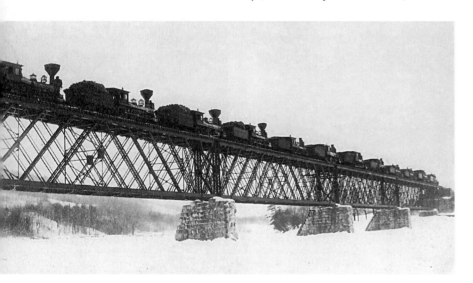

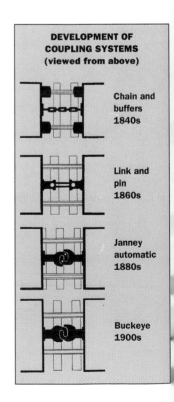

DEVELOPMENT OF COUPLING SYSTEMS
(viewed from above)

Chain and buffers
1840s

Link and pin
1860s

Janney automatic
1880s

Buckeye
1900s

shovels and the call for volunteers. Braking was a risky business, particularly in freight service. We did it by hand, as air brakes had not been invented. In bad weather, when it was snowing or, worse, sleeting, we put sand or ashes on the roof of the train to keep from falling off when we were moving from one car to the next. We had no footboards, or extensions at the ends of the cars, to help us from one to the other, and many times I have crawled along the top of a swaying boxcar, expecting each minute to find myself in the ditch. Automatic couplers were also something held in the grip of the future and the cars were fitted up with great wooden buffers.

"Accidents in which the train would split occurred when the engineer slowed for a curve, and the cars would charge up on him from the rear. When a break occurred it did not take the crew long to clamber on the roof and clamp down the brakes. Yet even these would not hold, the locked wheels sliding along the rails, carried forward by the momentum of the train. We had quite a few accidents that way."

The earliest brake, an iron wheel atop a shaft connected with the brake shoes on a car, was screwed down manually. On steep hills trains sometimes ran away.

The nineteenth-century woodburner *St. Lawrence,* converted to an inspection locomotive with a viewing gallery on the boiler and the bell moved back to the tender, patrols the Central Vermont Railway, later part of the CN system. The splendid carriage appears to be the mobile office of the senior inspector.

One of the worst accidents occurred in 1864 when the ill-fated *Ham* of the Grand Trunk crashed off an open swing bridge into a ten-foot canal at Beloeil, twenty-seven miles east of Montreal, killing the fireman, conductor, brakeman and eighty-three German immigrants and injuring another two hundred.

The Grand Trunk, one of the great railways of North America a generation before the Canadian Pacific was built, ran from tidewater at Portland, Maine, via Montreal and Toronto to Sarnia, Ontario, and eventually to Detroit and Chicago. Heavily travelled routes like that between Montreal, Toronto and Chicago, via Sarnia, Ontario, were double-tracked. By 1878 the Grand Trunk had 440 locomotives, 67 in passenger service and the rest in freight. It swallowed dozens of smaller lines, including the Champlain and St. Lawrence, and in 1882 took over the 853-mile Great Western Railway, which served communities between Toronto and the Michigan border. Along with the government-built Intercolonial Railway, which linked Nova Scotia, New Brunswick and Prince Edward Island to central Canada in 1876, it was part of the adventure in nation building that assured Canada's independence from the United States despite north-south pressures of commerce and culture almost as powerful then as they are today.

By the 1870s steel had replaced iron rails and the Grand Trunk had engines powerful enough to breach the thousand miles of forest, rock, lake and muskeg that blocked the way west. But when surveyors cautioned against building a line through the northern Ontario wilderness, the empty prairies and the Rockies, the Grand Trunk directors in London, England, were all too ready to listen. The honour thus fell to the Canadian Pacific, which reached Vancouver in the mid-1880s. Not until a quarter of a century later did a Grand Trunk subsidiary belatedly build a line across the West.

In 1880 Canada had 7,000 miles of track. Ten years later it had 17,657 miles, and the role the railways played in the minutiae of daily life, particularly in the countryside, would be hard to exaggerate. For a farm family a locomotive headlight across the night-cloaked fields assured them they were not alone under the wide prairie skies. Long before radio, the railway provided weather reports: discs on the sides of trains – a full moon for fine weather, a crescent for rain. After Sir Sandford Fleming's Standard Time divided the country into five time zones in 1884, farmers set their watches by the train. No longer did the Grand Trunk

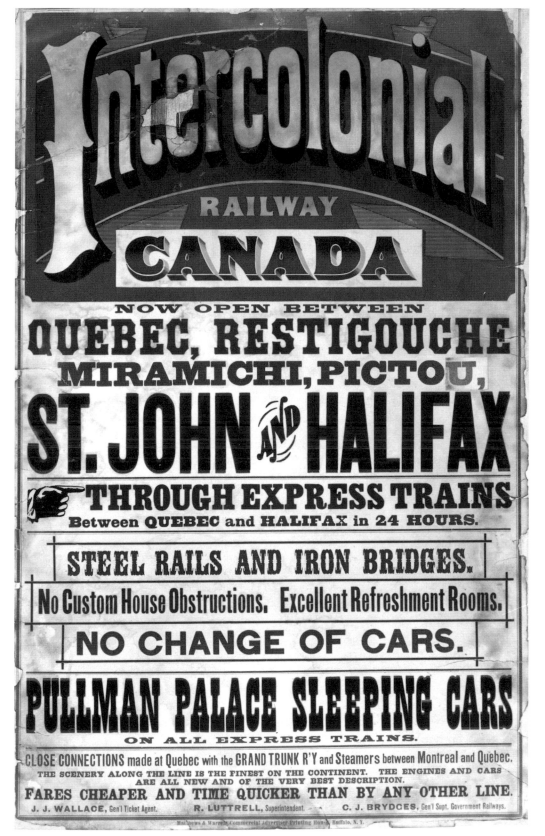

The Intercolonial Railway advertises through service between Halifax and Quebec City. The Intercolonial acquired the Grand Trunk line from Rivière du Loup, on the lower St. Lawrence, to Lévis, across the river from Quebec City, in 1879. Ten years later it acquired running rights into Montreal. This poster appears to have been patched, presumably to correct a spelling mistake in "Pictou."

Grand Trunk's No. 39 took to the rails in 1889 and ended life as CN 7097 in 1925. A yard switcher of the tank type, it carried its own water and coal so needed no tender.

timetable have to warn, "Trains will run on Montreal time, which is 12 minutes faster than Kingston time, 14 minutes faster than Belleville time and 25 minutes faster than Toronto time."

Clerks in a postal car on the head-end of a fast passenger train collected mail from stations en route and sorted it day and night for rapid delivery, and who is to say the system was slower than the one we have today? "It was twenty-two hours on shift by yourself working all the time, no sleep," recalled A. L. Robinson of British Columbia. "You're standing up and getting bounced around all the time."

Railways were the highways of entertainment, bringing famous singers, actors, lecturers and circus trains, including the hundred cars of the Ringling Brothers and Barnum & Bailey Circus, the "Greatest Show on Earth." Railways provided more modest entertainment as well, for if the church was the soul of small-town Canada, the railway station was its nerve centre. With its potbellied stove, wall clock, ticking telegraph sounder, neat garden and the name of the town spelled in white stones, the station drew people to hear the latest news, to bid a tearful farewell or a happy greeting to loved ones, or just to watch the world go by. Out on the tracks, youngsters had a ready-made if dangerous playground above the cinders, twirling the brake wheels atop idle boxcars, walking perilous trestles and dreaming of the day they too would be brave engineers.

When Moguls (so-named because the first models were sent to Russia in the mid-nineteenth century) were introduced, their 2-6-0 wheel arrangement was intended to power the heaviest freight trains. No. 893 was built in 1902, and by the time it was scrapped in 1931, heavier engines like the Consolidation had appeared and Moguls were relegated to light, fast freights.

Built in the 1850s and demolished a century later, Bonaventure Station was the main Montreal station for the Grand Trunk and CN until Central Station was opened in 1943. With its stained glass windows, pew-like benches and gas illumination, the waiting room in the 1870s was the epitome of Victorian elegance.

Steam trains rattled past backyards and sometimes right down Main Street, clanging and dinging amid startling bursts of steam. When the engineer turned the brass handle of the brake valve and notched out the throttle that fed high-pressure steam to the pistons, you could see the plunging rods drive the giant wheels. Unlike diesel locomotives, whose guts are hidden under metal skirts, a steam locomotive, with flaming firebox and aura of smoke and steam, was a show in itself.

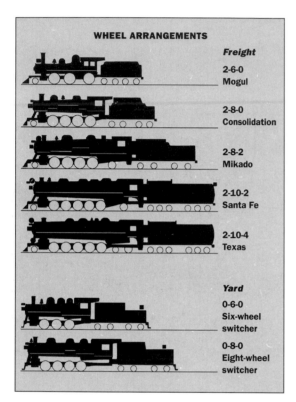

WHEEL ARRANGEMENTS

Freight
2-6-0
Mogul

2-8-0
Consolidation

2-8-2
Mikado

2-10-2
Santa Fe

2-10-4
Texas

Yard
0-6-0
Six-wheel switcher

0-8-0
Eight-wheel switcher

By the 1890s engine size had increased tenfold and trains were safer thanks to George Westinghouse's compressed air brakes, which appeared in Canada a few years after they were invented in 1867. They could be set simultaneously on every car by pulling a lever in the cab, which not only stopped the train faster but eliminated the need for several brakemen clambering about on top of moving boxcars. To keep a safe distance between trains, a manually operated system of signalling ensured that when a train entered a "block," which might stretch for a mile or more, no other train could enter until the first was out.

Passenger coaches, fifty feet long, were strengthened with steel and equipped with lavatories and tanks of ice water. Freight cars were carrying heavier loads, an economy of scale that helped contain the rising cost of transportation. More power was needed to haul the heavier trains at fifty or sixty miles an hour, and larger locomotives were popular with management, since no more men were required to manage a heavy train than a light one.

Bigger engines required trailing wheels for support. A typical passenger engine had a four-wheel lead truck, to support the front end and guide the engine around curves, and a two- or four-wheel trailing truck. The slower freight engines were built to place weight on the drive wheels for better adhesion to the track and had a two-wheel lead truck and a two-wheel trailer.

The 2-6-0 Mogul type, the biggest engine in the country when introduced in the 1850s, and the 2-8-0 Consolidation type, introduced in 1870 to haul heavy drags of freight, had begun a trend to more powerful freight locomotives, such as the 2-8-2 Mikado (so-named because early models were purchased by Japan) seen in Canada toward the end of the century. For dual-purpose freight and passenger service, the 4-6-0, known simply as the Ten Wheeler, became one of the most popular locomotives in the country. Adept at hauling ten or more passenger cars, considered large trains at the time, the Ten Wheeler remained common until the 1920s.

The steam engine spoke its own language, and to the fanciful its expirations were those of a panting beast. "You always had two exhausts coming," explained Alex "Beaver" Douglas of Thunder Bay. "That's what attracted people. The locomotive had two cylinders. The one working the right sounded just before that on the left, a pause that represented a quarter of a turn of the driving wheel." If the engine were not well tuned, one exhaust came stronger than the other, emphasizing the illusion of something alive.

WHEEL ARRANGEMENTS

Passenger

	4-4-0 American
	4-4-2 Atlantic
	4-6-0 Ten Wheeler
	4-6-2 Pacific
	4-6-4T Suburban
	4-6-4 Hudson
	4-8-2 Mountain
	4-8-4 Northern

There were nineteen signals a locomotive engineer might sound on his steam whistle during a day's work, the best known being the two long, one short, one long burst before one of Canada's thirty thousand level crossings, or the one prolonged blast that meant a train was steaming into a station. A whistle heard in Moncton, New Brunswick, was more or less the same in Vancouver, San Francisco or New Orleans, though engineers were known for their signature tunes. They might make their first blast slightly long, or a short one extra short, or leave a certain spacing, so their wives in the kitchen and friends in the station knew from their style who was at the throttle. On older locomotives with lower boiler pressure, engineers could control the pitch and intensity of the blast by varying the amount of steam going to the whistle.

The conductor in the passenger coaches communicated with the engineer by pulling the cord connected to an air whistle in the cab. Two whistles meant start the train; five meant increase speed. In acknowledgement the engineer blew two short blasts on the big steam whistle atop the engine.

Otherwise, there were forty distinct sounds peculiar to the steam locomotive, from the sibilance of a stack blower with the engine in repose to the *whomp-whomp-whomp* of air pumps as the engine came to ponderous life. Once the train was under way, the hum of the injector throwing thirty gallons of water a minute into the boiler and the hiss of the valve throwing sand from the dome to the wheels to stop slipping were drowned by the *choof-choof-choof* from the stack as the throttle was opened, and the hypnotic rhythms of a passenger train, *I think I can, I think I can, I thought I could, I thought I could,* syncopated with the *clickety clack* of the rail joints. The warning that steam pressure had risen too high was the automatic pop valve blowing off with a great *whoosh*.

Douglas V. Gonder, a foreman in charge of locomotives and later a CN vice-president, recalled the clatter of pokers and coal gates and the swish of escaping steam as a crew checked the locomotive of a heavy passenger train on a clear, cool night.

"Two flutelike notes from the signal whistle, and our engineer moves the brake valve handle to the running position. With a long, drawn-out and fading sigh, and perhaps a few creaks, the brakes release. With a *ssh*, the reverse gear goes to full forward, the headlight switch is turned on, and the dynamo's whine lowers a tone or two with the added load. The bell starts its clangour.

Foreman Nelson Germane at left leads a track maintenance crew to work near Dauphin, Manitoba, in 1908. Two men could pump the handcar at a good pace, but everyone had to join in to get it started.

"The throttle is opened and a hissing cloud of steam spits from each cylinder cock, one after the other, as we gather speed. Suddenly they are slapped closed and we hear the engine's muffled and deep-throated exhausts – four to every revolution of the wheels. Now the blower's strident hiss is stopped and the mechanical stoker's demanding steam jets take its place. Gradually the engine's exhausts come faster and faster and lighter and lighter as the reverse gear shortens the cutoff with a hiss each time it is moved. Soon we are rolling along at a good even clip, with snappy, even exhaust. The tires squeal as a curve is rounded. . . . Now and again the blow-off cocks roar as the engineer blows down the boiler. The whistle shrieks its warning at each crossing. There is a thrilling, throbbing babel of sound and we shout to be heard."

Steam locomotives were mechanically simple despite their juggernaut proportions; the two fundamentals were sufficient pull to get a load started and an adequate boiler to keep it going. The 4-6-2 Pacific type, introduced at the turn of the century to pull seven-hundred-ton passenger trains, fulfilled both these

Because of slow shutter and film speeds, sharp action shots of trains are rare before World War I. Although mostly crisp, the locomotive shows signs of blurring in this 1910 study of a Grand Trunk express train on the Montreal–Toronto double-track main line. Pacific type No. 202 was built in 1910 and became 5579 on the CN roster, enduring until 1960. Truss rods beneath the floors of the wooden baggage car and coaches stiffened the car bodies, but even then the cars creaked and groaned, and on rough track the floors could be seen to undulate. Boards placed across the rods provided a free ride for hoboes "riding the rods."

(Facing page) A Grand Trunk Pacific crew on the prairies in 1912 could lay three miles of track a day. In the top photo ties are brought up to the railhead. In the second photo a trainload of ties has pulled up behind the Pioneer tracklayer, which swings and places rails and ties for a hundred-man crew to spike down. The tracklayer was known as the "praying mantis" because of its odd shape,

The trestle at Wolf Creek is typical of the many bridges the Grand Trunk Pacific had to build as it pushed through the prairies and mountains to the West Coast. (British Columbia Provincial Museum)

At Zealandia, Saskatchewan, between Saskatoon and Calgary, a Canadian Northern train of nine freight cars plus caboose pauses to add loaded grain cars in 1909. In the decade since its founding, Canadian Northern had provided transportation for farmers in 130 western communities where the CPR did not run.

requirements, provided steam heat and light to the cars, and was adaptable to fast freight service.

Because of stock promotions and lavish government grants and construction contracts, it was always more lucrative to build railways than to run them. The frenzy of railway building that began in 1903, fuelled by an economic boom, inspired a new Grand Trunk manager in Montreal, a dapper, bearded little American named Charles Melville Hays, to follow the sun – and the rival Canadian Pacific Railway – by building to the Pacific Ocean. Laying track west from Winnipeg and north of the CPR line, the Grand Trunk Pacific created 120 new communities across the prairies and northern British Columbia. By establishing a terminal at Prince Rupert, British Columbia, a day's sailing closer to the Orient than Vancouver, the Grand Trunk Pacific hoped to steal a march on the CPR.

The Grand Trunk Pacific laid one of the best tracks on the continent, for Hays insisted on grades of no more than four-tenths of 1 per cent, which his chief engineer, C. C. Van Ardol, nicknamed "Four Tenths Van," pushed through the Rockies at Yellowhead Pass, west of Edmonton. At the same time, the federal government was building the National Transcontinental Railway, the Grand Trunk Pacific's eastern equivalent, from Winnipeg to Moncton through northern Ontario and Quebec. Though it ran through sparsely populated wilderness with little traffic, it was expected to pay its way by carrying western grain to eastern seaports and opening northern Quebec and Ontario to settlement, logging and mining. "Perhaps no more comprehensive plan of railway construction was ever conceived," said *Canadian Magazine* for April 1906. "It rivals the great Trans-Siberian Railway, undertaken by the Russian government, and the famous Cape to Cairo Railway which is to connect the two ends of the continent of Africa."

After survey parties, totalling a thousand men, had found their route, marking a three-foot-wide trail uphill and down across bogs, granite and forests with stakes planted every hundred feet, the contractors moved in men, horses, steam shovels, bog fillers and grading machines. Every three miles camps were established, and the work was divided into segments of twelve miles, each under the care of a civil engineer, aided by a transit man, rod man and chain man. They were charged with preserving the grade, ensuring the work was going to plan and keeping an eye on subcontractors, or "station men," who contracted to excavate or fill a certain length, or "station," of right-of-way. Dynamiting through the Shield or slogging through swamps, baking in July and freezing in December, the workers suffered hardships rarely encountered in peacetime. An awkward track-laying machine called a "praying mantis" brought up rails and ties, dumping them on the ground for men to hammer into place at the rate of two or three miles a day. A. C. Lipsett, who worked for the Grand Trunk Pacific when it was being built through Alberta, lived in a tent summer and winter. "There was no telegraph out there in 1912, so trains ran by smoke signals," he recalled. "The engineer looked ahead for smoke. If he saw any, he had his fireman put out a blast of smoke to warn the approaching engine."

Railways were the country's biggest industry, with their web of tracks, government grants of land as big as European principalities, thousands of locomotives, tens of thousands of freight cars and passenger coaches, their stock yards, handsome stations, teeming freight sheds, grimy roundhouses, docks, grain elevators, telegraph companies and ocean-going ships. Their luxurious parlour

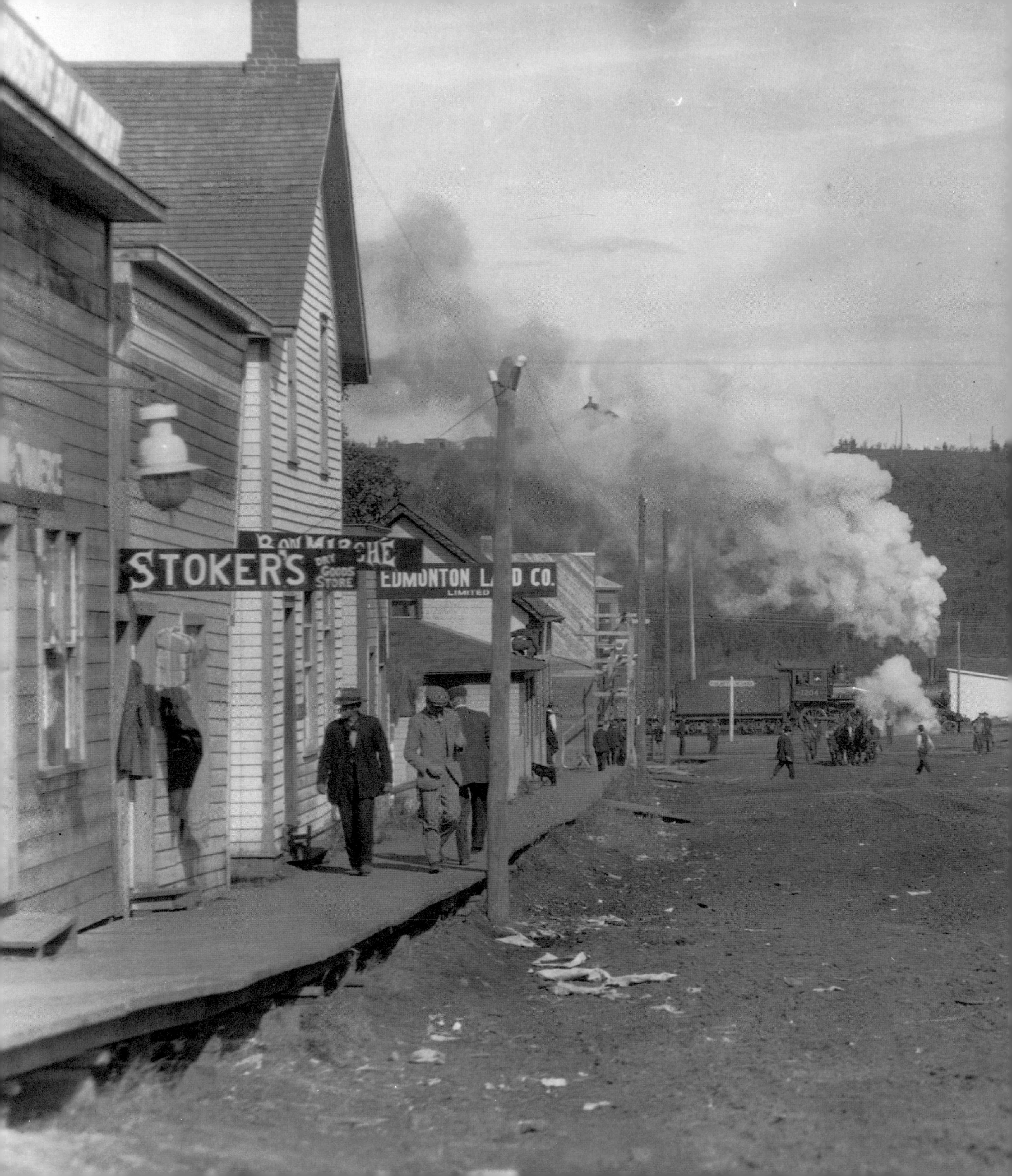
STOKER'S
DRY GOODS STORE
BON MARCHE
EDMONTON LA D CO.
LIMITED

By 1908 Canadian Northern had pushed eighty-eight miles from Hudson Bay Junction into the main street of the new lumbering and mining town of The Pas, Manitoba.

cars, dining cars gleaming with white napery and silver, darkened sleeping cars, and smoking compartments, with their aroma of good cigars and whiff of illicit liquor, brought to the countryside hints of sinful glamour in far cities. The dining rooms of chateau-like railway hotels were community and convention centres, the site of innumerable wedding receptions and Rotary meetings.

Like other great industries – lumbering, ranching, shipping – the railway evolved its own pecking order. The conductor was responsible for ensuring that the train moved according to orders from the dispatcher. In the cab, the engineer was in charge of motive power, assisted by a fireman, who in the days before automatic stokers was the hardest worker on the train, shovelling tons of coal per shift to keep steam up.

Once a tried-and-true method ensured that the trains ran on time and in safety, there was great reluctance to change it. "As with the army, so with the railway," said the December 1920 issue of *Canadian National Railways Magazine*, "certain conditions are essential to the formation of the close-knit organization. . . . One essential is unquestioning obedience to orders. We have to assume that the officer who gives them knows why, and that it is in the best interests of the organization of which he commands a small part that they be carried out."

Apart from running trains, the railways assumed roles usually filled by government. They sent agents to Europe to recruit immigrants to colonize the Clay Belt of northern Quebec and Ontario and the wheat fields of the prairies, "Canada's thousand mile farm." Even so, railway construction outpaced population growth. This was particularly true when Sir William Mackenzie and Sir Donald Mann, two former backwoods Ontario schoolteachers who became self-made railway barons, built a third railway to rival the Grand Trunk and the CPR. Starting in piecemeal fashion in the 1890s, they built their Canadian Northern Railway, based first in Winnipeg and later in Toronto, into a line that stretched across Canada. On the eve of World War I Canada possessed nearly 35,000 miles of track, a mile for every 250 inhabitants, compared with a mile for every 400 in the United States.

The first two decades of the twentieth century were the golden years of steam. Automobiles were in their infancy and highways primitive or nonexistent. Everyone, it seemed, was riding the rails, and the railways were all things to all men – and women. When the Duchess of Connaught, in the governor

general's private car, complained that water slopped out of her bath, engineer G. A. Fenby of Edmonton recalled having to stop the train for fifteen minutes every morning while the Duchess took her bath. (Fenby, a railroader for forty-six years, also drove the pilot train that went ahead of the royal train carrying the present Queen Elizabeth in 1951.) Railroading was celebrated in song and story, the most famous figure being John Luther "Casey" Jones, who took "his farewell trip to the promised land" when his southbound *Cannonball* piled into a freight train on the night of April 30, 1900, in Mississippi. But generally railways were safer than ever before, due to better brakes and steel coaches having replaced wood.

A derailment on the Grand Trunk at Sarnia, Ontario, circa 1912. The locomotive is a 2-6-0 Mogul type built by the Grand Trunk in 1889. It survived this episode and went on to service with CN, being retired in 1927. (Ontario Archives)

Between 1875 and 1900 there were more than 750 fatalities and 2,100 injuries on Canadian railways. Automatic air brakes introduced late in that period reduced spectacular derailments like this pileup on the Intercolonial in Nova Scotia, though they do not seem to have helped in this case. (Courtesy John S. MacRae)

Even so, the fear of accidents loomed large. Conductor A. J. Elliott of Toronto said that after a derailment at Cobourg, in which cars of coal overturned, he found a man's boot on top of the coal and feared someone was buried. After much digging and moving of coal, no one was found.

Fireman George T. Harrison, who began his railway career in 1908 in Manitoba, recalled a freak accident one night on westbound passenger train No. 1 out of Portage la Prairie when they ran into a tornado. It blew an empty boxcar sitting on the incline of a nearby siding into the locomotive, part of it landing on the cab. "Fire blew back out of the firebox. I grabbed a shaker bar and dumped the fire. The boxcar caught fire. We climbed onto the tender and got buckets of

water to quench it. The engineer had a cut over one eye. If the boxcar had been laden, we would all have been killed. None of the passenger cars was damaged."

The vigilance of telegraph operators did a great deal to reduce accidents. D.S. McCready of Jasper was a Grand Trunk Pacific telegrapher at Mountain Park on a line that ran to the coal mines south of Edson, Alberta, when he saw a locomotive moving past his station. A few minutes later a hostler, who controlled the engine when it was being serviced, rushed into his office and said that an inebriated brakeman, who had long dreamed of becoming an engineer, had climbed into the engine, opened the throttle and taken off down the line.

"What to do?" said McCready. "If the brakeman was not too drunk to run the

The Canadian Northern logo, adopted by CN for a short time, was superseded by the Grand Trunk logo style when that railway was assimilated into CN in 1923.

Two variations of the Grand Trunk logo. The one above appeared on Grand Trunk Railway system timetables in eastern Canada up to 1923. The other is from a 1910 Grand Trunk Pacific timetable when service was extended west to Edmonton.

engine out, perhaps he was not too drunk to bring it back." It was decided to send a section crew and the hostler to follow in a handcar. They came upon the engine standing still fifteen miles out of Mountain Park and persuaded the brakeman to hand over the controls to the hostler.

In 1913, their peak year prior to World War I, Canada's trains carried 106 million tons of freight and 46,230,000 passengers. Nevertheless the Grand Trunk Pacific, which though privately owned had been heavily financed by government, was dragging down its parent, the venerable Grand Trunk. The Canadian Northern was in crisis. So long as it had remained a regional western railway of three thousand miles, it had prospered. But Mackenzie and Mann, caught up in the prewar fever of expansion and not wishing to build a system that might lack sufficient capacity as soon as it was finished, had overextended themselves with tracks totalling ten thousand miles.

Everything came to a head at once. World War I cut off the British financing. Immigration and settlement dried to a trickle. And when the Grand Trunk and the Canadian Northern faced bankruptcy, the federal Conservative government felt obliged to take them over and combine them with money-losing railways owned by the government. In the discouraging climate of inflation and economic depression after the war, the government began to mould this disparate assortment of railways into Canada's first national crown corporation.

Big Business, represented by St. James Street in Montreal, predictably called this an unacceptable intrusion into private enterprise. There had been precedents, however, the government having created the Intercolonial Railway in the 1870s and the National Transcontinental in the early 1900s. Some 220 different companies – railway, shipping, hotel, telegraph and express – went into the mix to form Canadian National Railways, including Canadian Northern, the Grand Trunk Pacific, the National Transcontinental Railway, the Intercolonial Railway and their various subsidiaries. The last to join was the eldest, the Grand Trunk Railway, in 1923.

CN's first president, David Blythe Hanna, the Scot who ran the daily operations of the Canadian Northern while Mackenzie arranged the financing and Mann laid the tracks, began putting Canadian National Railways together in the recession that followed World War I. He said in his memoirs, *Trains of Recollection*, "It was fated that we should carry through one of the strangest phases in the history of transportation – to change two great systems of privately projected and privately controlled railway into public ownership properties."

CN's operating ratio had deteriorated from 95.6 per cent in 1918 to 114.5 per cent two years later, meaning it cost nearly $1.15 to earn a dollar. "It is a heartbreaking affliction," said Hanna, "to have to go on month after month with the results of a ceaseless endeavour written monotonously in red ink."

Since the rival Canadian Pacific had a well-established passenger service, with world-famous ships and luxury hotels and fine cuisine, Hanna concentrated on freight. Always the bread and butter of Canadian railways, freight earned at least 75 per cent of railway revenue, and despite the recession the government authorized CN to buy 8,450 new freight cars and 163 locomotives "for the purpose of getting freight traffic."

In favouring freight over passengers, Hanna was a generation ahead of his time, for in the Canada of the 1920s passenger trains were still needed. Not only were cars and buses few and far between, but so were roads. There were hundreds of communities whose only contact with the outside world was the CN track.

In any event, Hanna, who had become CN's president in 1919, had little time to pursue freight. Following a change of government, the Liberals ousted Hanna in 1922 in favour of a newcomer to Canada, Sir Henry Thornton, hired by Prime Minister Mackenzie King. Thornton, who had made his name in passenger service, had plans more ambitious than Hanna's – plans that would fashion the future of Canadian National Railways for a quarter century.

(Overleaf) A Canadian Northern Railway train powered by a Consolidation type, a heavy freight locomotive whose 2-8-0 wheel arrangement was long favoured by CN, which inherited eight hundred from predecessor railways in 1923. The first "Consol" model appeared in 1866.

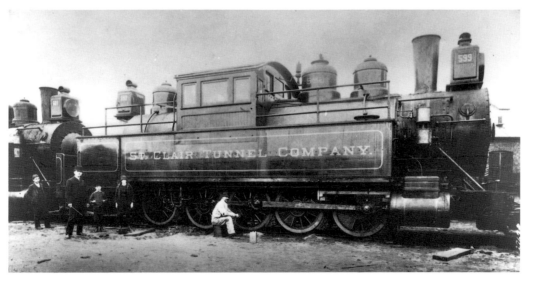

When the St. Clair Tunnel between Sarnia, Ontario, and Port Huron, Michigan, was opened in 1891, hardy little switching locomotives operated in either direction without turning. If they stalled in the tunnel there was danger of crew suffocation. In 1920 they were replaced by electric locomotives.

Crowds see off a Grand Trunk troop train at Toronto in World War I. Steel rails were the backbone of the war effort, though the upheavals of the war also contributed to the failure of many of the great lines that later went to make up CN. (City of Toronto Archives)

The Grand Trunk Railway built stations to last. The station at St. Mary's Junction, today preserved as a heritage building, was constructed of stone in 1856 when the main line opened between Stratford and London, Ontario.

2

THE PEOPLE'S RAILWAY

On January 31, 1923, Canadian National Railways took over the Grand Trunk Railway, long the dominant line in Quebec and Ontario. In five years CN had ingested five major rail systems and with them the dreams, achievements, mistakes and debts of seventy years of railroading.

With 22,646 miles of track, CN was a third larger than the CPR. Nor was CN simply a railway, for like the CPR it owned large tracts of land, and it operated nine hotels and two lodges, a fifty-thousand-mile commercial telegraph system and ships in both oceans. If its 3,265 locomotives, 3,363 passenger coaches, 124,648 freight cars and 6,544 cabooses and work cars were linked, they would have stretched from Halifax to Toronto.

Since Canadian National and Canadian Pacific were now providing 90 per cent of Canada's railway service, Canada was unique in being served by competing private and public systems. But whereas the CPR had been purpose-built for profit, CN had the task of uniting five former competitors, including government lines built to fulfil social and political policies, into one viable system.

CN had inherited so much debt from its component companies that it was obliged to pay exorbitant interest. It had also inherited two or more sets of everything – staff, stations, repair shops, telegraph lines – and hundreds of miles of duplicate tracks. Fifty per cent of its track needed repair and some in the West was too light for 1920s traffic. Operating standards, locomotive types and rolling stock were often incompatible and there was little team spirit. Crews rolling into

The single semaphore paddle tipped upward dictates that Mountain type No. 6017 must take the rails to its left and around the curve at St. Henri toward Victoria Bridge, Montreal.

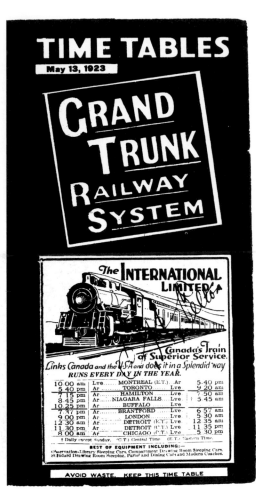

Cover of Grand Trunk timetable, May 13, 1923.

Detail from back cover of
Grand Trunk timetable, May
13, 1923. The menu shows
how tastes in food have
changed since the 1920s.

Montreal from the west still called themselves "Canadian Northern," while those from down east were still "Intercolonial."

Critics called CN the National White Elephant but its new
president dubbed it "the People's Railway," the slogan of the Intercolonial, and vowed to give Canadians an organization they could
be proud of. For Sir Henry Thornton, the empty northern tracks of
the former National Transcontinental were an asset, a key to the
wealth of minerals, forest resources and hydroelectric power of the
north.

Thornton moved the headquarters from Toronto to the Grand
Trunk building on McGill Street in Montreal and painted a vision
of railroading rarely seen since that other larger-than-life American, Sir William Van Horne, built up the CPR in the previous century. Unlike the traditional railway chieftain who had worked up
from teen-aged apprenticeship, Thornton was a new breed. Before
gaining experience in many departments of the Pennsylvania
Railroad, which claimed to be the best on the continent, he had
taken a degree in civil engineering. In an industry that normally
promoted by age and seniority, he managed to become a division
superintendent at the age of thirty.

At forty Thornton was running the Long Island Railroad's commuter service into Manhattan's Penn Station. At forty-three he went to England
to restore the Great Eastern Railway to leadership in London's commuter service.
In World War I, as an acting major general, he organized troop trains to the front
lines in France, for which he was knighted. He was fifty-one when recruited to
head the Canadian National Railways after others had turned down the job as impossible. "I like a good fight, and here was the place to have it," he said.

It was not always a fight. As a crown corporation CN could call on more
government funding than even the CPR had enjoyed. CN could count on the support of Canadians who opposed a CPR monopoly – particularly prairie farmers
who had helped build Canadian Northern as a counterweight to the CPR. He
had inherited a seasoned pool of professionals, and trains that could cross
Canada without having to run into the United States, as the CPR had to between
Montreal and Saint John, New Brunswick. In Yellowhead Pass west of Edmon-

ton CN enjoyed the easiest western mountain grades of any railway in North America.

To bring the sprawling giant under control, Thornton split CN into three regions, Atlantic, Central and Western, each under a vice-president, and the regions were divided into forty-four divisions and 120 subdivisions. The western leg of the old Grand Trunk, in Michigan, Illinois and Thornton's native Indiana, became a CN subsidiary, the Grand Trunk Western.

The future lay in expansion, said Thornton, whose style matched the times. During the next six years, while Canada basked in a prosperity unknown since before World War I, CN and the CPR fought for supremacy, to the advantage of the travelling public if not the public purse. CN advertised as lavishly as its private enterprise rival and competed in excellence of meals and service. Both railways refurbished their grand hotels, built new stations, and created two of the best passenger services in the world, though passengers accounted for only 15 per

Superannuated boxcars were bunkhouses, kitchen and diner for this CN maintenance crew improving the right of way in the Fraser Valley in 1931. Canadian Northern Railway logos are still discernible.

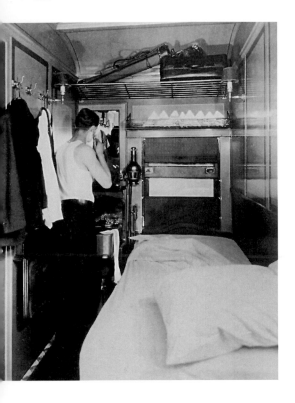

Shaving on a moving Pullman car could be a harrowing experience, no doubt partly responsible for the invention of the safety razor. In this 1927-model single bedroom, the sink was beside the bed, the toilet in a separate compartment.

cent of CN's revenue. The Roaring Twenties – and for those who still had money, the Dirty Thirties – was a glamorous era for North American railways. Hollywood made movies about railways and Tin Pan Alley wrote songs.

CN had ordered few passenger coaches since World War I. Thornton ordered 3,500 units of rolling stock, mostly for freight, but also including first-class coaches with interiors of mahogany veneer and seats of olive-green plush. Some were decorated with rare hardwoods from Madagascar and finished in antique English oak that was so handsome it was neither stained nor varnished but simply polished. Lounge cars were finished in maple veneer and had a sunroom at one end, and some included a barbershop, a tile shower, a soda fountain and an innovative public telephone service. Sleeping cars were finished in dark mahogany, upholstered in grey, blue and brown, and named for Canadian cities, celebrities and ports.

Massive steel passenger cars, built to travel great distances and withstand Canadian winters, were so much more imposing than the smaller trains of Europe that people crossed the Atlantic just to ride Canadian "landliners" across the prairies and Rockies. While neither the world's fastest nor most luxurious, Canadian trains were rarely exceeded for comfort. The comfort extended to CN's senior officers, who were supplied with seventy-three ornate business cars equipped with bedroom, dining room, bathroom and kitchen. (The railway also operated four private cars for the prime minister and his cabinet and two for the governor general.)

Demonstrating that CN was "more than just another common carrier," Thornton had been on the job only six months when he introduced a service unknown on other railways. Setting up transmitters in cities along its route, CN broadcast symphony concerts, plays about Canada's history, children's programs and hockey games to eighty lounge cars on sixteen main-line trains. "Radio-equipped observation cars had an aerial right on the roof," recalled Jack Carlyle of Toronto, who helped establish the service. "They installed thirty-two headphones at the seats and a loudspeaker operated by an attendant." Hailed as the first radio network in North America, the system was sold to the government

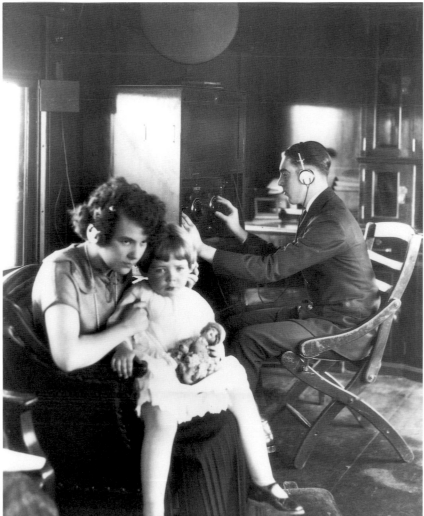

CN pioneered radio entertainment on trains in 1923. Studio and transmitting equipment of CN's radio station CNRW were crammed into a colonist car (above) on a siding at Winnipeg. Programs were picked up by passenger trains and broadcast in parlour cars over earphones or loudspeakers. In the second photo, an operator twiddles dials in 1925 to provide passengers with music, drama, children's programs and sports broadcasts. The CN radio network, the first in North America, became the basis of the Canadian Broadcasting Corporation.

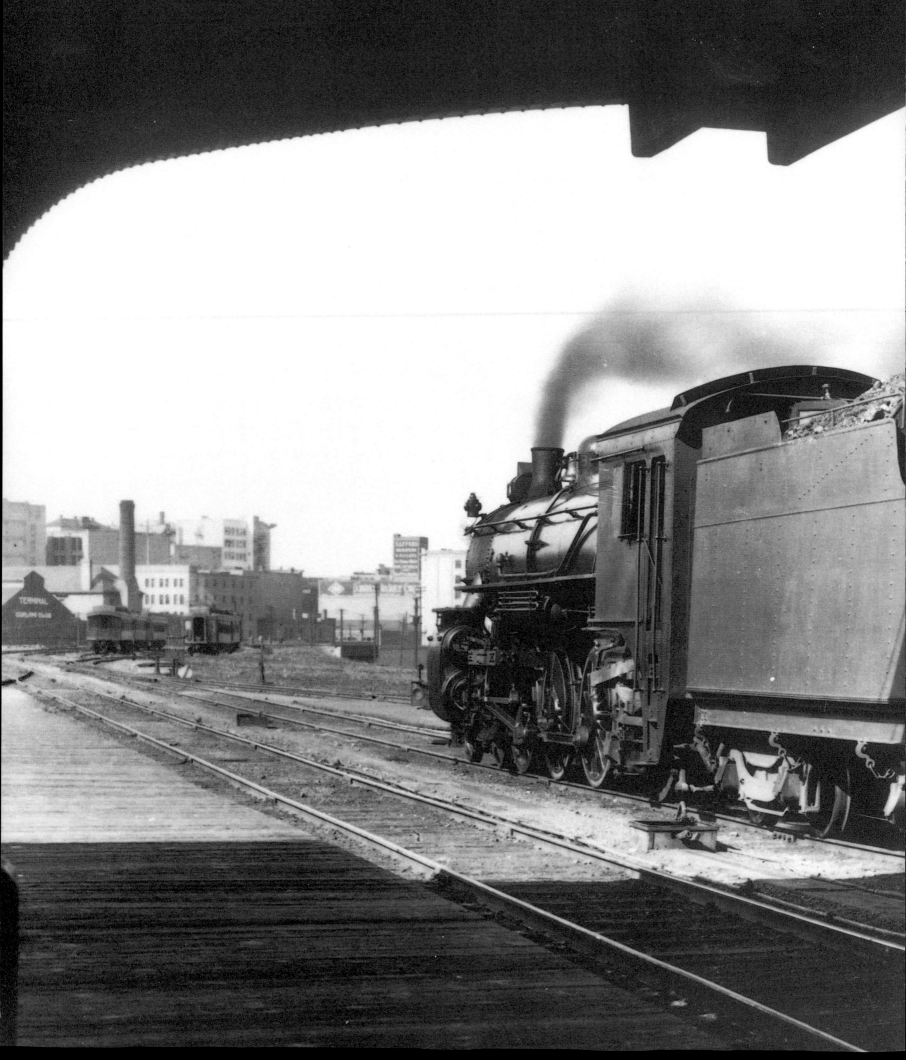

Framed by the canopy of Winnipeg's Union Station in 1920, a local passenger train, hauled by a Pacific type, waits for the conductor to pull the communication cord twice to signal the start of another journey.

One of CN's 334 fast Pacific type locomotives accelerates away from Vaudreuil, near Montreal,
in 1930. The Intercolonial Railway introduced the type to haul heavy passenger trains in 1905,
three years after the first Pacifics appeared on the Missouri Pacific Railroad in the States.

during the Depression and became the foundation of the Canadian Broadcasting Corporation.

Whereas the affluent CPR had led the field in modern locomotives, CN now challenged its rival, as North America entered the last great age of steam. Engines had changed little in profile since the 1890s, and although no new types were invented in the 1920s there were improvements in efficiency. Increasingly bigger and more powerful, locomotives pulled longer trains at higher speeds. Before World War I the average weight of a steam engine, not counting the tender, had been less than 100 tons. The average now was 200 tons, and CN's biggest freight locomotive, the 2-10-2 Santa Fe type, acquired to haul heavy freight on steep grades near Toronto, weighed 325 tons. Though there were mightier engines, notably the 4-8-8-4, 132-foot, 400-ton Big Boy in the States, Canada's "battleship on wheels" was the most powerful in the British Empire.

Though CN continued to rely on eight hundred inherited 2-8-0 Consolidations, it scrapped what Thornton described as "seven solid miles of useless, discarded locomotives." Six hundred engines were retired, including sixty-year-old "tea kettles" now too light for main-line work. For freight service CN ordered the latest version of the 2-8-2 Mikado. For passenger service it favoured the 4-6-2 Pacific. CN also introduced the dual-purpose 4-8-2 Mountain type. Its superheater reduced loss of pressure between boiler and cylinder and its automatic stoker – a steam-powered conveyor between tender and firebox – meant the engineer no longer had to depend on the muscles of the fireman to shovel eighteen tons of coal at 133 shovels per ton. All-weather cabs replaced drafty, leaky cabs with flapping canvas curtains.

Thornton was not content with improving steam engines. During his years in England he had heard about the Swiss and Swedish railways' experiments with Rudolf Diesel's internal combustion engine. Since diesel engines were new to North America, he sent his vice-president of operations, Samuel J. Hungerford, and his young chief of motive power, C.E "Ned" Brooks, overseas to find diesel engines that might work on the railway. At the Beardmore works in Glasgow, Scotland, they found a diesel engine which, though it was originally designed to power the propellers of dirigibles, they used to power self-propelled diesel-electric rail cars to compete with automobiles and buses on light-traffic branch lines. Rail cars were economical since they dispensed with standard crews and conventional trains.

Though the cars looked like glorified streetcars, one of them, No. 15820, made history in 1925 by travelling 2,937 miles in sixty-seven hours of running time from Montreal to Vancouver, twenty hours faster than the regular steam passenger train. Another, with thirty-seven passengers, sped nonstop from Montreal to Toronto in a record-breaking five and a half hours.

In 1928 CN produced a more substantial diesel electric, No. 9000, one of North America's first successful road diesels. Apart from its boxlike body, it was much like locomotives built today, with a diesel generating plant that supplied electricity to motors geared to the axles. Its twin unit, No. 9001, joined it a year later, and together they measured ninety-four feet, weighed 303 tons and could reach speeds of eighty miles an hour. For the next twenty years, because of the Depression, financial woes and the premature death of Brooks, CN did nothing to

A historic moment as CN's pioneer diesel No. 9000, on a test run in 1929, takes to a siding to let ten-year-old Mikado type No. 3348 go by. This is one of the earliest photos of a Canadian steamer passing a diesel.

capitalize on its breakthrough. Apart from acquiring small yard engines, which were often more efficient than steamers in marshalling freight cars, it relinquished the lead in diesel design to the United States.

No. 9000 was tested in 1929 hauling the seven-car *International Limited* from Montreal to Toronto. "The 9000 was a great reward for the efforts of a mechanical genius," said H. J. "Herb" Palmer, the engine driver on its test run. "Upon my arrival next day at the shop I told my fellow engineers that the diesel locomotive was, in time, going to replace the steam locomotive. The boys said it was all nonsense."

Steam locomotives being the ultimate form of railway traction in the mind of the times, CN's forceful vice-president Starr Fairweather believed the potential of steam had yet to be fully realized, and CN built more than seventy steamers in

When they were introduced in the early 1920s, ninety-foot-long Mountain types were CN's most powerful motive power, though a few years later that distinction went to the big Santa Fes. The engineer of 6020 is ringing his bell with a cord in this 1932 photo. Later the bell was rung by air pressure.

the late 1920s in its shops at Montreal, Moncton and Transcona, near Winnipeg, which in 1926 produced the first steam locomotives built in western Canada.

In 1927 CN began a thirty-three-year love affair with the 4-8-4 Northern type, introducing the 6100–6400 series a few months after the Great Northern Railroad had introduced the design in the States. Since the Northern appeared on Canada's sixtieth birthday, the first in the series was initially named the Confederation type. CN was to acquire 203 Northerns, more than any other railway. Well suited to hard winters and long distances and meeting a demand for lighter axle loadings, it could handle both ninety-car freight drags and sixteen-car passenger trains and was tailored to CN's needs by the Canadian Locomotive Company, Kingston. Billed as "super-locomotives," early models achieved speeds of eighty-five miles an hour and later models got up to a hundred. They were economical, only one Northern being needed to haul the *Ocean Limited* the 841 miles from Montreal to Halifax, whereas other types had to be changed three times en route. Frequently improved over the years, the Northern type was CN's principal engine in central and eastern Canada until its honourable retirement in favour of the diesel locomotive in 1960.

Speed was of the essence, said Thornton, though he didn't particularly enjoy fast trains himself in his constant travels around the system. To break the CPR's

Cutaway diagram of a 4-8-4 Northern type locomotive.

Firebox interior showing:
• staybolts, which separate boiler shell from firebox
• brick arch to direct fire path

Boiler interior showing firetubes, which carry hot gases through boiler water

Smokebox interior showing:
• petticoat pipe extending down from chimney
• exhaust steam nozzle below it
• firetubes exiting into smokebox

Cylinder interior showing:
• spool valve in upper chamber to control steam flow to lower chamber
• piston connected to driving gear

(Above) CN's largest silk train, twenty-seven cars in two sections, being made up on the Vancouver docks, 1927. Pulled by the fastest engines, like this Pacific passenger locomotive (left), more than a hundred CN "silkers," averaging ten to twelve cars, made the 2,749-mile dash to New York between 1925 and 1932. (Upper photo: Vancouver Public Library)

forty-year monopoly on Asian trade, CN started fast silk specials out of Vancouver. Insurance was so costly and the National Silk Exchange in New York so volatile that delay might mean heavy losses for the shipper in Japan. The trains were guarded by CN police, and when a winter blizzard clogged the tracks CN could marshal battalions of men to shovel the drifts so a silker could thunder through.

CN had found a route whereby it could rush the silk to the States hours faster than the CPR, and its trains sped 2,749 miles across Canada, green lights glowing all the way, via Toronto to the border at Niagara Falls, whence the New York Central Railroad whisked the silk to market in New York. Two weeks before the silk arrived by ship at Vancouver, dispatchers across the country were warned that "every minute possible must be saved." Packed in 130-pound burlap sacks, the first CN cargo of silk to leave Vancouver was bundled off a ship on July 1, 1925 into eight insulated express cars lined with paper against dirt and splinters. Though some "consists" were only three cars, one consisted of twenty-seven cars in two sections which left Vancouver in October 1927. L.E. Scott of White Rock, British Columbia, recalled riding a silk train on the thirty-mile downgrade into Melville, Saskatchewan. "I believe we were doing well over ninety miles an hour, because small stones were sucked up onto the rear platform."

R. H. Davis of *Railroad Magazine* was riding CN's *Confederation* when it was sidetracked at Armstrong, Ontario, to make way for a silk train of twenty-one cars in two sections. "A whistle screamed, as out of the dark, the headlight shining along the glistening rails, thundered Section One with its precious cargo. The brakes groaned, the engine whistled, and the silk special brought up with tremendous clanking. A new engine replaced the hot monster that had come through the last 147 miles; the train crew gave way to a fresh detachment, the cars were watered, the brakes inspected, the locks in each car examined by special officers, and in exactly four minutes Section One was on its way."

Jean G. Coté, of the dispatcher's office at Edmonton, recalled standing near the signal tower one evening, hearing the whistle of a distant silk train and seeing it thunder past him two minutes later in the wintry twilight. "The engine raised a cloud of cinders, clattering away over the diamond," said Coté. "Soon only the twin red eyes of its last car-marker lights were visible." During the next sixteen years, before silk was replaced by synthetic fibres, CN ran a total of one

Although it is a provincial capital, Fredericton had to be content with a CN branch off the main line between Moncton and Montreal. Locomotive 1241, one of several daily trains, was a diminutive Ten Wheeler built for Canadian Northern in 1907.

Railways made prairie grain a major export product. The annual harvest called for extra manpower from the East, and the railways offered "Harvest Excursions" at a penny a mile for anyone who would work for a few weeks in the grain fields. This photo shows relations bidding farewell to harvesters heading west from Union Station, Toronto, in 1922. (Metropolitan Toronto Reference Library)

hundred silkers. Some travelled from Vancouver to New York in eighty-four hours, though the average was slightly less than ninety-one hours, half a day faster than the fastest passenger schedule. The average silk train carried four thousand bales of raw silk, worth $400,000. Pound for pound, silk was the most lucrative cargo.

By 1925 CN was carrying more freight than its rival and competing neck and neck for passengers. When Thornton took over, four crack trains inherited from predecessor companies, three of them "Limited," meaning they made a limited number of stops and had limited accommodation, were the pride of the passenger fleet. *The Continental Limited* from Montreal and Toronto to Vancouver had entered service in December 1920, the *Ocean Limited* had been inaugurated by the Intercolonial between Montreal and Halifax in 1904, and *The National* had been plying between Toronto and Winnipeg since 1914. The doyen of the fleet, and one of the best trains on the continent, was the *International Limited*, which had been running a fast luxury service between Montreal, Toronto and Chicago since it was inaugurated by the Grand Trunk in 1900.

During Thornton's decade, twenty-eight new passenger trains were added. They included *The Confederation* from Toronto to Vancouver, *The Acadian* from Montreal to Halifax, *The Ambassador* between Montreal and Boston, *The Maple Leaf* between Montreal and Chicago, *The Montrealer* and *The Washingtonian* between Montreal and the American capital, *The Chicago Express* from Toronto, and *The Inter-City Limited* between Montreal and Chicago via Toronto.

(Facing page) With Mount Robson, the highest peak in the Canadian Rockies, as a backdrop, a Pacific type pulls *The Continental Limited* in 1930. The line had been built by the Grand Trunk Pacific a generation earlier with easier grades than the Canadian Pacific Railway had to contend with two hundred miles to the south. In the photo at left, the train pauses for five minutes at Mount Robson Station in the 1940s so passengers can admire the spectacular view. Observation car 15100 was assigned to the Yellowhead Pass run between Jasper, Alberta, and Kamloops, British Columbia.

(Upper left) Grain wagons unloading at the Co-op elevator, Rhein, Saskatchewan, on a branch line near Yorkton. A passenger train is getting up steam in the background. Since the 1970s trains on some western routes have tripled to thirty a day, with the average train increasing from fifty to eighty-seven cars. This bridge (left) at Clarkesboro, Saskatchewan, is still strong enough to support the traffic a century after it was built.

To increase efficiency and safety, electrically controlled automatic block signals had replaced manually operated signals. Having laid fresh ballast and heavier rails through northern Ontario, CN stole a march on the CPR in 1927 by achieving a better running time between Montreal and Winnipeg with *The Continental Limited.*

Travellers having become impatient with changing their clothes in berths four feet high, CN revolutionized the Canadian sleeping car, introducing en suite washroom and lavatory. Its new dining cars seated thirty-six people and measured eighty-seven feet. Its lounge cars had twenty-three reclining chairs and a sun lounge.

To serve the growing wheat market, the railways webbed the prairies with three thousand miles of branch line, two-thirds of it CN rail. Every September armies of men rolled west in colonist cars for the grain harvest; thousands of

The prairie farmer was one of CN's best customers. At Rosetown, Saskatchewan, famous for grain production, locomotive 326 picks up boxcars on the line between Saskatoon and Calgary.

In the Dirty Thirties, Shawinigan Falls, Quebec, was a busy mill town with frequent train service and a new station at a time when services were being reduced in many other regions. This photo was taken just before the station opened. The train order board is still mounted on the old building closer to the camera, used as a temporary depot during construction. Notice the horse-drawn wagons at the platform.

boxcars were marshalled to carry export grain to the West Coast and through
Winnipeg to Thunder Bay or to Quebec City and the Maritimes. To export
wheat via the shorter shipping route from Hudson Bay, CN in 1930 completed
the railway the federal government had been trying to build since 1910, laying
the final seventy miles to Churchill, Manitoba, over permafrost. Three trains a
week, two freights and a mix of freight and passengers, ran to Churchill.

In the 1930s CN helped to open northern farmland to the unemployed of the Great Depression. When a train arrived at Lois in the Abitibi region of northwest Quebec, sleighs stood by to take settlers to their wilderness homes.

The two-thousand-mile National Transcontinental line which stretched
through northern Quebec and Ontario to Winnipeg, and which had seemed
such a hopeless national extravagance when its last spike was driven in 1915,
was beginning to generate revenue as lumber and pulp-and-paper mills sprang up
and gold-mining communities flourished at Pickle Lake, Red Lake and Crow
Lake, and copper-mining at Rouyn.

"The CPR no longer bestrides Canada like a Colossus," observed the *Canadian*

Forum. "Another great railway system has been built up, largely on the strength of government contributions, to curb the giant's power."

"Our only motive," protested Thornton, "is to make our railway the People's Railway, of real service to the people of Canada." Recalling that immigration had fuelled the turn-of-the-century boom, and wanting to populate land granted to CN predecessor companies, he established a Department of Colonization and Agriculture with government authority to "select, transport and locate suitable immigrants for permanent settlement in the Dominion." Like the CPR, CN brought in tens of thousands from England and Europe, advised them where to settle and helped them select their cows and horses.

Living up to its motto as the "People's Railway," CN ran medical, dental and school cars. Children of loggers, trappers, Indians and the sectionmen who maintained remote stretches of track came in canoes in summer and on snowshoes in winter to attend the School on Wheels.

Fred Sloman, son of a Grand Trunk Railway baggage master, inaugurated a mobile school that was hauled up and down forty-eight miles of track between Capreol and Foleyet in northern Ontario, bringing education to children who otherwise would have never known a schoolroom. Supported by the provincial government, CN ran four school cars and the CPR two, fitted with desks, blackboard and living quarters for the teachers. From 1926 until they retired in 1964, Sloman and his wife taught in mobile schools, bringing education to a thousand children and night classes to their parents

Adept at public and employee relations, having learned from the publicist Ivy Lee at the Pennsylvania Railroad, Thornton was the antithesis of the aloof railway boss of Victorian times. He went out of his way to meet people at their work, sometimes visiting yards at night.

Seed grain was delivered to St. Felicien, Quebec, in 1930 by the carload and measured out to the settlers by filling sacks through a grain door. The man in charge is no doubt the chap with the clay pipe. In the second photo, sheep are loaded aboard cattle cars for shipment to market in 1927.

Hungarian immigrants change trains in Toronto for the west in 1927. CN's Department of Colonization and Agriculture played a leading role in recruiting settlers, who were 85 per cent of
CN's passenger business from Europe in the 1920s.

The old colonist cars were still in use after World War II, when hundreds of immigrant trains bearing Europeans displaced by the war travelled from the port of Halifax to the Canadian west. In this 1950s photo the immigrants were on their way to Manitoba.

Canadian National Railways

This herald (the term railway people used before the word logo entered the language) came into use in the between-the-wars period.

"In the early days of railroading it was very rare, indeed, when a conductor or brakeman had the honour of meeting a higher officer," former conductor D. J. McMillan said at the time. "As for meeting the president, to see him was a red-letter day indeed. To my mind, a wonderful change has taken place, for the present management is a most democratic one, and in my opinion herein lies the secret of the success achieved."

Thornton introduced scientific management, overhauled a pension system inherited from the Grand Trunk, and formed a company-union co-operative for non-operating workers. The Union-Management Co-operative Movement first appeared at the CN shops in Moncton and spread across Canada in the shops and among maintenance-of-way and express and telegraph workers. "When I started working at CN there were no paid holidays except things like Christmas. No week's vacation," said Richard W. Worraker, a general foreman at Point St. Charles. "It was Sir Henry who started them, through the Union-Management Cooperative meetings."

In 1928 CN did so well that it seemed about to become the financially self-sufficient railway Thornton had promised. As well as using a large amount of coal for its own engines, CN was moving considerably more of the nation's coal than its rival. Coal was its single most lucrative freight. The wheat crop that brought Canadian railways so much of their income broke all records. Mackenzie King wrote warmly in his diary of Thornton's "originality, real ability, broad vision and courage" and concluded he was the right man for the job. By 1929, six years after he had taken office, Thornton had tripled income and built CN into one of the great railways of the world. It was operating 24,000 miles of track in Canada and the United States, compared with 17,000 by the CPR. While his success was due in part to luck – the economic boom of the Roaring Twenties – it was also due to his knowledge of railroading, attention to employee relations and his gift for publicizing a railway that had suffered too long from a Cinderella complex.

"A railway's work is never done," said Thornton, and modernized *The Confederation*. The fastest passenger engines available, five clean-lined 4-6-4 Hudson type steamers of the 5700 series, were assigned to the Montreal–Toronto leg of the *International Limited*. The Hudson cut running time from Montreal to Toronto to six hours, saving almost an hour and a half. A Hudson, with its eighty-

A CN school car (above) at Capreol in northern Ontario in 1926. The children, who lived too far from towns to go to ordinary schools, arrived on snowshoes or skis.

(Left) Fred Sloman is the travelling teacher on this school car in northwest Ontario. The son of a railroader, Sloman pioneered classes for children who otherwise would have had to depend on government correspondence courses.

When coal was king. Until 1960 most steam locomotives were powered by soft coal from Nova Scotia and the foothills of the Rockies. Hauled out of Drumheller, Alberta, by two yard switchers, these coal-filled boxcars begin their journey to dockside at Thunder Bay, whence lake steamers will carry the coal to eastern Canada and the United States.

inch driving wheels, pulled *The Inter-City Limited* to set a steam locomotive record in 1930, covering 334 miles in 360 minutes.

Until the autumn of 1929 Thornton, like Sir Edward Beatty of the CPR and most businessmen, had operated as if prosperity had come to stay. Though CN's long-term debt had doubled since Thornton's arrival, in a time of plenty Ottawa had agreed to CN's expenditures with little or no question. As the Depression took hold, however, CN had to reduce expenses. Only a third of its tracks were profitable. Passenger trains, freight branch lines, ships and hotels all began to lose disastrous amounts of money. With 101,000 employees, compared with the CPR's 70,000, Thornton reluctantly ordered layoffs.

Thornton's critics accused him of mismanagement and extravagance, and the accession of a Conservative government precipitated his downfall. The Conservatives used him as a convenient punching bag to discredit the Liberals; the Liberals did little to defend him. It is hard to avoid the conclusion that Thornton was a scapegoat, but he had also made mistakes. In building so enthusiastically,

Door-to-door delivery. A fleet of horse-drawn wagons line up on the cobblestones at the freight depot near Bonaventure Station, Montreal, in 1927.

(Above) Ticket counters at Union Station, Toronto, were built of brass and marble. In 1927 clerks had preprinted tickets in the rack for the most popular destinations.

(Top left) Segregation of the sexes for women travelling alone was common in railway waiting rooms like this one at Kamloops, British Columbia, in 1927.

(Left) Winnipeg's Union Station was nine years old in this 1929 photo. More than seventy years later, as a Via Rail Canada station, it looks much the same after restoration of classic detail.

CANADIAN NATIONAL RAILWAYS
BUFFET CAR SERVICE

GRAPE FRUIT (½), 30c   BAKED APPLE, 15c; WITH CREAM, 25c
STEWED PRUNES WITH CREAM, 30c
ORANGE JUICE, (2), 35c   ORANGE WHOLE, 15c; SLICED 20c
SLICED BANANA WITH CREAM, 25c
CEREALS WITH MILK, 20c; WITH CREAM, 30c
OLIVES, 20c   CHOW CHOW, 15c   MIXED PICKLES, 15c
CONSOMME SOUP, 30c   VEGETABLE SOUP, 30c   CREAM OF TOMATO SOUP, 30c
IMPORTED SARDINES, 50c   DOMESTIC SARDINES, 25c
FISH (In Season), 70c
(See Special Slip)
INDIVIDUAL CHICKEN PIE "NATIONAL," 85c
CLUB STEAK, $1.00   LAMB CHOPS (1), 45c; (2), 85c
CALF'S LIVER with BACON, 65c   PORK CHOPS (1), 50c; (2), 95c
BACON (3 strips), 35c; (6 strips), 65c   HAM (full cut), 65c
HAM (½ cut) OR BACON (3 strips) WITH FRIED EGGS (2), 65c
EGGS: BOILED (1), 20c; (2), 35c   FRIED (1), 20c; (2), 35c
POACHED ON TOAST (1), 20c; (2), 40c   SCRAMBLED (2), 35c
OMELETTES: PLAIN (3), 45c
PARSLEY, CHEESE OR TOMATO (3), 50c
JELLY OR HAM (3), 60c
BAKED PORK AND BEANS, 35c
COLD HAM OR OX TONGUE, 75c   WITH POTATO SALAD, 90c
BOILED OR MASHED POTATOES, 20c
HASHED BROWNED OR COTTAGE FRIED POTATOES, 25c
CANADIAN PEAS, 20c   FRENCH PEAS, 30c   STEWED TOMATOES, 20c
SUGAR CORN, 20c
SALAD: HEAD LETTUCE, 45c   SLICED TOMATO, 45c
(With French or Mayonnaise Dressing)
PRESERVES, etc.
(In Individual Jars)
ORANGE MARMALADE, 15c   ASSORTED JAMS AND JELLIES, 15c
PRESERVED FRUITS, 25c   HONEY, 25c   PRESERVED FIGS, 40c
INDIVIDUAL DEEP APPLE PIE WITH CREAM, 30c
ENGLISH PLUM PUDDING, WITH HARD SAUCE, 30c
ASSORTED BISCUITS, 20c
CANADIAN CHEDDAR, FRENCH ROQUEFORT OR CAMEMBERT
CHEESE, TOASTED CRACKERS, 30c
SANDWICHES: HAM, 25c   EGG, 25c   TONGUE, 25c
WHITE, GRAHAM OR FRUIT BREAD WITH BUTTER (4 slices), 15c
HOT ROLLS OR CORN MUFFINS, 15c
DRY OR BUTTERED TOAST, 15c
TEA (per pot), 25c   COCOA (per pot), 25c   COFFEE (per pot), 25c
MALTED MILK, 20c
INSTANT POSTUM (per pot), 25c
INDIVIDUAL SEALED BOTTLE SPECIAL MILK, 15c
Afternoon Tea Service 3.30 to 4.30 p.m.
No order served for less than 25c to each person.
Waiters are strictly forbidden to take or serve verbal orders.
Guests will confer a favor by requesting meal order blank.

It will be appreciated if patrons will report any unusual service or attention
on the part of employees of Sleeping, Dining and Parlor Cars, to Superintendent
at Montreal, Que., as this will enable the Management to recognize exceptional
efficiency, which we desire to encourage in our service.

WALTER PRATT,
General Manager,
Montreal

A menu from 1928.

he had equated Canada's growth potential with that of his native American mid-west. He had made questionable purchases, such as the Scribe Hotel in Paris, without clearing them with Ottawa. Though he knew more about the mechanics of railroading than his opposite number at the CPR, who had reached the president's chair from the law office, he lacked Beatty's grasp of finance. As the *Montreal Star* said, "He was a great railwayman. He was a great politician, but he was not too good at counting his small change." He had made enemies in high places, but his ultimate enemy was the Great Depression, as it was for so many others.

In the summer of 1932, ailing and heartsick, Thornton was maneuvered into resigning by R. B. Bennett's transport minister, Dr. R. J. Manion. The following year Thornton died a broken man at the age of sixty-two in a New York City hospital. Few politicians attended his funeral, but Thornton was mourned by tens of thousands of CN employees. In fifteen railway stations across the country they paid him the unique honour of erecting bronze plaques in his memory.

For three dismal years, while Beatty did his best to have CN incorporated into the CPR, the People's Railway struggled on under a government-appointed Board of Trustees headed by a former chairman of the government's Board of Railway Commissioners, Judge C. P. Fullerton. Business was half the level of 1928. The government instructed CN and the CPR to form a Joint Cooperative Committee to cut duplication, which resulted in the pooling of passenger trains in the Quebec City–Toronto corridor. One of the first trains to be pooled was the Montreal–Toronto leg of *The Inter-City Limited*, which usually made the run with a consist of nine cars.

Only the trunk lines, such as those from Montreal and Toronto to Vancouver and Halifax, were paying their keep. Morale sagged as people were laid off. Any

The upper deck of the graceful bridge across the Niagara Gorge carries an eight-car CN international train into Canada in 1929. The first bridge on this site was opened in 1855 by the CN predecessor company, the Great Western Railway.

A Northern type, the pride of CN steam power, pulls the royal train bearing the Prince of Wales
to open Toronto's Union Station in 1927. Though the station had been completed in 1920,
disputes over routing had delayed the official opening. (National Archives of Canada)

expense over $25,000 had to be vetted by the trustees. Though Samuel Hungerford had succeeded Thornton to the office of president, he was confined to operating day-to-day service much as he had as vice-president. The big decisions were made by Fullerton, and to do him justice he fought to maintain CN's independence when pressures were exerted to amalgamate CN with the CPR.

When the Liberals returned to power late in 1935, with the economy already improving, C. D. Howe, the new minister of transport, dismissed the trustees in order "to restore management by experts in the railway business." Hungerford, chairman now as well as president, waged a vigorous campaign to restore CN to economic health. Passenger trains were equipped with mechanical air conditioning and lighter dining cars. To bolster freight trade, CN acquired modern refrigerator cars and forty-ton express cars, which looked like boxcars but had passenger car trucks for speed.

CN produced Canada's first semi-streamlined locomotives, a development of the Northern type, designed in collaboration with the National Research

The *Prince Henry* was one of CN's fleet serving Seattle, Vancouver, Prince Rupert and Alaska. In this 1931 photo a train meets the steamer at Prince Rupert, built by the Grand Trunk Pacific before World War I.

(Overleaf) The afternoon flyer from Toronto arrives at Hamilton's new station in 1931. First off the baggage car is the *Toronto Daily Star*, being loaded onto trucks. The Royal Mail from the first car behind the locomotive gets less rapid handling into a horse drawn wagon.

Council. They had such innovations as a rounded nose, streamlined cowl and running board apron, but the louvres installed beside the stack to direct smoke away from the cab were of dubious value. This handsome series in green and gold passenger livery began regular service between Montreal and Toronto and also powered VIP trains. In 1939, with the royal coat of arms under its headlight, No. 6400 hauled the blue and silver royal train of twelve cars that carried King George VI and Queen Elizabeth for part of the four thousand miles on the final eastbound leg of a tour that aroused royalist and patriotic emotions unheard of today. Later that year one of these modernistic engines went on exhibition at the World's Fair in New York.

The year 1939 was a turning point in the annals of the People's Railway. Having weathered the amalgamation of five ailing components, the poverty of the Dirty Thirties, and the threat of being swallowed by Sir Edward Beatty of the CPR, who had now retired, CN was to play a heroic role in World War II.

Because of the Depression, CN and the CPR began pooling passenger operations in April 1933 in the heavily travelled Quebec City, Montreal, Ottawa and Toronto corridor, ending the fierce competition of the 1920s. The *International Limited* in the olive-green and gold livery of CN and tuscan-red of the CPR is leaving Montreal's Windsor Station in 1937 behind a CN Hudson.

The parlour car had overtones of an exclusive club. Swivel seats permitted group conversation or, when turned to the window, a degree of privacy, with push buttons to summon the porter. Air conditioning, provided by chunks of ice stowed in insulated boxes (left), was common by the mid-1930s. Ice was cut from rivers and lakes and stored in sawdust-filled sheds to await warm weather.

Celebrating the hundredth anniversary of public railways in Canada. (Above) Steam whistles of both locomotives sound off as Winnipeg railroaders cheer the anniversary. (Below) A replica of the Champlain and St. Lawrence Railroad's *Dorchester*, which in 1836 was the first locomotive to haul a passenger train in Canada, poses beside a new streamlined 6400.

(Facing page) The five partially streamlined Northern type 6400s which CN bought in 1936 pulled fast passenger trains in southern Quebec and Ontario until they were replaced by diesels in the 1950s. These photos show how they looked before and after the shrouding was fitted. Among CN's 2,448 steamers in the early 1950s, eleven were streamlined.

(Facing page, top) In the 1920s skiers discovered the Laurentian slopes via the CN line "up north" from Montreal. CN ran regular ski specials like this one at St. Sauveur in 1939.

(Facing page, below) Pioneer diesel locomotive 9001 built in 1928 pulled passengers in southwest Ontario until World War II. One of the first main-line diesels in North America, it is seen in its black and gold livery in 1937 bound east toward Toronto's Union Station.

Freight paid the bills. The patient task of collecting and delivering freight cars on sidings across the country fell to switching crews with powerful little yard locomotives like the 0-6-0 type No. 7453 switching at the Montreal grain terminal in 1939.

3

OUT OF
STEAM

ORLD WAR II GAVE CN A NEW LEASE ON LIFE. WITH HIGHWAY TRUCKING
in its infancy, the materiel and manpower of war were carried by rail. Taking advantage of thousands of miles of surplus track that had been the "railway prob-
lem" for a quarter century, CN became as essential to the war effort as the army,
navy and air force.

Rust-streaked track through northern Quebec and Ontario shone bright
again under the wheels of hundreds of freight and troop trains rolling east to
waiting ships. Barely three months into the war CN passed its first wartime test.
In forty-eight hours it dispatched twenty-five trains to Halifax with the van-
guard of the Canadian First Division bound for Britain. When the *Ocean Limited*
to Halifax had to add six sections to handle wartime traffic, CN created a new
name-train, the *Scotian*.

On government orders CN marshalled eight special commuter trains a day
carrying twenty-thousand workers to munition plants. Wheat from the prairies
flowed to eastern ports through the northern wilds of Ontario and Quebec in a
volume the builders of the National Transcontinental had dreamed of but never
achieved. After the Panama Canal was closed by Nazi submarines, 2,500 flatcars
were mobilized to carry British Columbia timber destined for the United King-
dom via eastern Canadian ports.

Designed to handle heavy freight and masses of people, the railway converted to war more readily than most industries, but the long years of the Depres-

Built at the Alco plant in
Schenectady, New York, in
1918, Mikado No. 3518
spent most of its life hauling
freight on the Grand Trunk
Western, though the majority
of CN's large fleet of "Mikes"
was dispersed across
Canada. Notice that the let-
tering "Canadian National"
has been machined off the
number plate. The steam
coming from beneath the
cylinders is being exhausted
to carry with it condensed
water that would cause cylinder damage.

Soldiers line up with their kits at Halifax in 1939 after disembarking from their troop train.

sion had taken their toll. Bridges had to be strengthened, underpasses enlarged and switches changed to accommodate "circus trains" with loads of outlandish size – tanks, naval guns and tugboats. Rolling stock dating from the Boer War and hidden away in weed-grown back lots was retrieved and rebuilt. Freight cars and Northern type engines were purchased, but otherwise every aging piece of equipment was worked to the limit. The seventeen-year-old No. 6028, a Mountain type, was pushed so hard that it set a record by averaging 592 miles a day for a month, hauling *The Continental* between Toronto and Armstrong, Ontario.

With a dozen trains and seven hundred boxcars required to load a single cargo vessel, the speed of the average train was doubled, the average load of the boxcar was increased from thirty-five to forty tons, and freight trains ran to unprecedented length, sometimes one hundred cars. "We had to get that stuff down to the ocean ports and get it to hell over to England and France if we were going

Colonist cars were pressed into service as World War II troop trains. Each section of four seats had a removable table and food was fetched from a kitchen car that might be six hundred feet away.

to win the war," said fireman Ken Leathem of Ottawa. "There were a lot of times when we worked sixteen-hour days." Added his friend Frank Lapointe, "Some of the engines were antiques; breakdowns were frequent."

At CN's biggest roundhouse, at Turcot Yard near Montreal, teams of boilermakers and fitters worked all the hours in the week to keep tired engines running. With fifty-six stalls, Turcot Roundhouse repaired and groomed as many as 145 iron horses a day, sending them back to work in two to three hours.

"I sometimes wonder how they moved as much stuff as they did, under the conditions they did," said J. L. "Jack" Cann, a maintenance engineer and later a vice-president of operations. "On the main line west of Montreal's Turcot Yard I used to see traffic piled up caboose to engine, nose to tail, for five and ten miles. The trains were running with the frequency of streetcars."

CN's first wartime crisis developed when eastbound freights and troop trains clogged the funnel from Moncton to Halifax, and coal and steel trains from the mines and mills of eastern Nova Scotia bound for central Canada tried to squeeze past them. Trains were sidetracked for hours before they got a green light. Expensive double tracking, such as that between Montreal and Toronto, would have taken too long and steel rails were hard to obtain in wartime. With no time to lose, CN settled for a cheaper alternative, Centralized Traffic Control (CTC), a vast improvement on the automatic block signal system of the 1920s. CTC had been used in the States for some time but in Canada only on a spur line at Quebec City.

When Centralized Traffic Control was introduced in the Maritimes, a dispatcher in charge of 125 miles of track between Moncton and Truro sat at an eleven-foot console in Moncton, read the location of trains from a recorder, and activated distant switches and red, yellow and green signals by remote control. While not as efficient as double tracking, CTC allowed twenty trains to highball down to Halifax with a safety margin of only a few miles between them.

By 1942 Japan had stretched CN's war effort to the Pacific coast. Prince Rupert, which had been stagnating for years, became the busy port envisaged when the Grand Trunk Pacific was built half a century earlier to tap the riches of the Orient. Traffic increased from six to sixteen trains a day when the American army, finding western Canada's rail network a better route than the sea passage, made Prince Rupert a springboard to Alaska, filling little-used tracks with freight and troops from Chicago and Seattle. When the Japanese invaded the Aleutians, No. 9000, the pioneer diesel built in 1928, was draped with steel plates and assigned to a seven-car armoured train to protect the right-of-way on the line to Prince Rupert.

The Northern Alberta Railway, operated jointly by CN and the CPR before CN took it over completely, was transformed from a grain conduit between Peace River and Edmonton into a five-hundred-mile supply route for building the Alaska Highway. Edmonton, like Halifax a CN town, joined that east coast port as a hectic centre of the war effort.

R. C. Vaughan, former vice-president of purchasing and stores and Hungerford's successor as chairman and president, reported that CN was fulfilling its promise to carry record loads of people, munitions and the products of farm and factory. CN was hauling 50 per cent more freight than in 1928, its peak peace-

time year, and carrying two-thirds more passengers. *The International Limited*, which had normally consisted of nine cars, was sometimes running six sections between Toronto and Montreal. For the first time in a dozen years CN was making money, having reduced operating ratio to 77 per cent, the lowest in its history.

In July 1943 CN opened the Montreal Central Station which the Canadian Northern had envisaged when it pushed its tracks under Mount Royal to the centre of the city. Thornton had begun work in 1928 on this replacement to the Grand Trunk's old Bonaventure Station, but construction had been halted by the Depression and people had taken to calling the unsightly excavation "Thornton's folly." The new building, which the railway advertised as "one of the most modern station buildings in the world," had none of the grandeur of Union Station in Toronto, but no railways were building cathedral-like stations any more. Six and a half million people and 35,000 trains passed through in its first year.

A heavy freight train passes a trainload of tanks at Debert, Nova Scotia, in 1942 en route to Halifax and a convoy bound for Britain. Debert, some seventy miles from Halifax, was a major army staging camp.

(Overleaf) In 1939, locomotive 6162, a three-year-old Northern type, leaves the turntable at Turcot Roundhouse, Montreal, to pick up *The Maritime Express* for late-morning departure for Halifax.

Before World War II CN employed fewer than twenty women in its motive power and car equipment department. Annabelle Cooper, seen here in 1943, was CN's first female crane operator, hired in the late 1920s at the Battle Creek, Michigan, shop of Grand Trunk Western. At the time CN employed twenty female ticket agents, but its other four thousand women were stenographers or telegraph operators. During the war, more than nine hundred women worked as labourers, oilers and crane operators. In the second photo, one of them cleans the driving gear of a locomotive at the Toronto roundhouse.

(Preceding pages) Mobilized for war. Locomotives on the "ready track" at Turcot Roundhouse, Montreal, await crews to roll them to their trains in 1939. An old-fashioned roundhouse, it was always a smoky, steamy place and became more so in winter with condensing steam.

To carry the wartime flood of passengers, new coaches and locomotives were added. Twenty semi-streamlined Mountain type locomotives, "Bullet Nosed Betties" capable of averaging sixty miles an hour, were assigned to *The Continental Limited* and intercity trains. Otherwise, the railway was short of virtually everything – locomotives, boxcars and passenger cars.

Though many steam locomotives in western Canada had been converted to take advantage of Alberta oil, coal consumption had doubled across the system. CN burned so much coal during the war – thirty-six million tons – that deliveries lagged and half a dozen passenger services had to be cancelled. Boxcars for prairie wheat were so scarce that makeshift grain storage depots were set up in ice rinks and community centres.

With fourteen thousand employees in the armed forces, the "home guard" shouldered extra work and women were hired as never before. While women had been 17 per cent of Canada's labour force before the war, only 3 per cent had been in railway service, as stenographers, clerks, telegraph operators and a few coach cleaners. A rarity had been Annabelle Cooper, who made history at CN's Grand Trunk Western shops in Battle Creek, Michigan, as a crane operator.

In a revolutionary measure inspired by the needs of war rather than gender equality, women became ticket agents, chefs, waiters, engine oilers, welders,

Tank cars at the Imperial Oil Refinery in east Montreal, 1944. When highways, trucks and pipelines were in their infancy, railways transported the fuel for war.

Making good use of hundreds of miles of rail that had lain virtually idle in peacetime, the railway became the backbone of Canada's war effort. Here a wartime freight running westbound at St. Lambert, east of Montreal, stretches to the horizon with crated materiel. CN carried twice as much freight during World War II as it had in its best peacetime years.

A clean locomotive functioned best. High-pressure steam blasts dirt and grease from the running gear of this Mountain type locomotive at Spadina Roundhouse, Toronto, in 1946. CN introduced Mountain types in 1923.

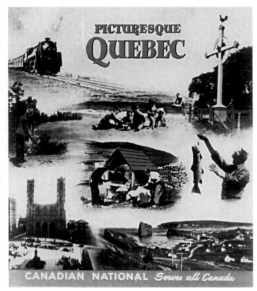

Brochures and posters promoted passenger travel and accommodation at CN hotels. These designs date from 1946.

lathe operators and labourers. At Stratford, Ontario, CN hired thirteen female machinist's helpers, five painters, two plumber's assistants, two electricians, a sheet metal worker and Canada's only female blacksmith. Though there were a thousand skilled female blue-collar workers at CN, the cab and caboose would remain a totally male preserve for another generation. Most of the women in blue-collar work gave up their jobs after the war to returning veterans.

Peace was an anticlimax. As highways, airports and pipelines sprouted across the country, railways were no longer undisputed kings of transportation. Government-controlled freight rates remained low in deference to the Maritimes and the West with coal and wheat to sell. On the other hand, operating costs rose so high that CN was having to haul several hundred tons of coal before it made enough margin to buy a ton of the stuff to fuel its fires. After five war years of heroic railroading, CN relapsed into prewar deficits.

Both CN and CPR suffered from lack of a coherent national transportation policy, but as a crown corporation CN had the additional burden of regional development. The small and unprofitable local railways it had been required to rescue had been a minor burden compared with the cost of renewing the struggling Newfoundland Railway and Steamship Service when Newfoundland joined Canada in 1949.

The seventy-year-old, 706-mile Newfoundland Railway was the only narrow-gauge line in Canada and the longest in the world. Its major train was the *Caribou*, affectionately if ironically nicknamed the "Newfie Bullet" because it took so long to travel the 547 rugged miles from St. John's to Port-aux-Basques, with coaches, dining car and sleepers. Except in the war years, the Newfoundland Railway had lost money, and its forty steam engines and many of its one thousand freight and passenger cars needed replacing. Bridges and right-of-way required improvement, and the pay of four thousand employees had to be increased to match that of CN workers on the mainland.

Operating now in all ten provinces under a patriotic maple leaf logo and the motto "Serves All Canada," CN maintained 5,000 stations, 7,000 bridges,

The *Caribou*, or "Newfie Bullet," leaves Port-aux-Basques for St. John's, Newfoundland, 547 miles and more than twenty hours away. In 1967 the *Caribou*
was replaced by buses, and twenty-one years later the railway was closed
down in favour of highway transportation. Long before it was part of CN, the
Newfoundland Railway adopted CN's tilted square (right) as the basis for its
logo. This example dates from 1943. In 1949, it began to be supplanted by
the CN maple leaf.

A refrigerator car chilled by ice is unloaded at a team track, a term that endured long after
motor trucks had replaced the teams of horses that brought drays to railway sidings.

121,000 freight cars and 3,500 passenger cars. The Blue Folder, CN's eighty-six-page timetable, listed 1,400 separate schedules. Its tracks south of the border – the Grand Trunk Western, the Duluth, Winnipeg and Pacific Railway, the Central Vermont and CN's line to Portland, Maine – totalled 2,600 miles in eleven states, from Maine to Minnesota.

Most of CN's 2,400 steam locomotives were thirty to forty years old and many were rebuilt veterans of the 1920s. Since 1929 the railway had bought only 322 new steamers, the last being twenty bullet-nosed Mountains in 1944. Starr Fairweather and his research and development department had failed to increase the thermal efficiency of steamers to compete with diesels and now advised president Vaughan to begin nationwide dieselization.

The steam car ferry *Huron* plied the St. Clair River from Windsor to Detroit for many years, carrying freight and passenger cars between CN and Grand Trunk Western rails. The passenger connection was replaced by a bus in the mid-1950s but the ferry continued to move loads too high or wide for the St. Clair Tunnel.

Facing page, top) Two new diesels in 1949 pull a heavy freight past Cobourg, Ontario, bypassing the spout that would continue to water steam locomotives for another decade. The gilded fronts of these diesels did not last beyond the next order, being replaced by cheaper golden-yellow paint.

Facing page, bottom) A twelve-car freight passes Grenadier Pond on the main line west of Toronto. Mikado 3380 is one of a hardy series of sixty built for service in northern Ontario in 1918 with vestibule cabs against rough weather.

Though CN had perfected North America's first successful diesel road engines, Nos. 9000 and 9001, two decades earlier, it had not pursued its advantage, and U.S. railways had taken a ten-year lead in 1935 when General Motors Corporation began mass production of diesel locomotives. By the end of the war three thousand diesels were working main lines in the United States.

Up to 1947 Canadian railways had confined diesel engines to switching duties but now they began to catch up. CN assigned six road diesels to main-line freight service between Montreal and Toronto and experimental diesels appeared on *The Continental Limited*, though as late as 1950 steam locomotives still hauled 90 per cent of Canada's trains. The first CN area fully dieselized was Prince Edward Island, where the steam locomotives needed replacing, coal was costly, and the self-contained nature of the island made it suitable for experimentation.

A diesel locomotive cost three times as much as a steam engine, but it was cheaper to maintain and its fuel cost less than coal. Though it developed massive power its controls were lighter and easier to handle and it could stop faster than a steamer. Whereas steam engines converted only 7 per cent of fuel energy to traction, diesel-electric generators, turning energy into power to feed motors on the drive wheels, converted 25 per cent.

Steam locomotives needed fuel and water every 125 miles or so, whereas a

The gas-electric motor train, known as the doodlebug, jitney or gas car, was an economical substitute for a branch-line train of locomotive, coach, express car and baggage-smoking car. Trailing two coaches, a motorized express-baggage car crosses the Miramichi River near Newcastle, New Brunswick, in 1950 while two maintenance men shelter on the safety platform.

Until covered hoppers appeared in the 1950s, a grain car was simply a forty-foot boxcar with inner doors to contain the cargo. The inspector tests grain for cleanliness, moisture and mildew.

2,500-horsepower diesel could haul a hundred-car freight five hundred miles without refuelling. A diesel could cruise at eighty miles an hour, and while not necessarily faster than a Northern type steamer, it made fewer stops and thus better time. Though two or three steam engines might combine to pull a heavy drag, each cab required a crew. With the versatile diesel, as many units as necessary – perhaps as many as six or eight – could be linked with a single control system, requiring one driver for all.

"Steam engines were a challenge to keep hot, and it took an awful lot of people to operate them," said Graham Crossman of Saskatoon, who drove them for a dozen years before switching to diesels. "The diesel was a big money saver." It was cleaner, pulled more cars and was soundproofed to cut track noise and the roar of the diesel plant behind the cab.

Nevertheless, many veteran engineers remained loyal to the steamer and found diesels monotonous. "With a heavy freight diesel you could pull your throttle out to number eight position and your road regulator would look after it from there," said Lorne Brisbin of Belleville, Ontario. "With a steam engine, an engineer had to exert initiative and expertise."

An old engineman told him, "Lorne, the company is wasting money on those things – they'll never last." When Brisbin asked him why, he replied, "I don't know. They just don't *look* like an engine." Whereas each steamer had its own individuality and generic name, the blunt-nosed, slab-sided diesel was mass-produced and identified, like a robot, by impersonal letters and numbers, such as the GPA-17a No. 6508 built in 1954 for *The Continental Limited*.

"The first diesel came down to this part of the country in 1950," said Webb Vance of Moncton. "Somebody said, 'Don't worry about that. It's just a fad. It will never work down here – the winters will kill it. It's not heavy enough. There are too many breakdowns.' Well as we know it wasn't just a fad, and in a few years the steam engines were on their way out."

Alex "Beaver" Douglas of Thunder Bay loved the drama of steam, but accepted that diesels were here to stay. "We lost the romance," he said. "We had all figured diesels would never be any good but they were. Much better than we anticipated and getting better all the time. Big machines, big tonnage. Time marches on. They were safer. They didn't have boilers that could blow on you, but you could get electrocuted on the diesel train. You were running with six hundred volts in the cab of the diesel."

Dieselization was just getting under way in 1949 when R.C. Vaughan retired, to be succeeded by Donald Gordon. Though a banker by training, the new boss of CN was called "Dieseling Donald" by the press as he threw his public relations skills behind the total conversion.

The first fully dieselized passenger train was the *Ocean Limited* in 1954; the following year CN introduced *The Super Continental*. While Gordon did not usually emulate Sir Henry Thornton in costly competition with the CPR, the "Super" was a notable exception, introduced to compete with the CPR's famous *Canadian*. Though CN had to travel 2,930 miles compared with the CPR's 2,881, both trains took the same time, seventy hours east and an additional forty-five minutes travelling west. Each "Super" was hauled by two GPA-17 General Motors diesel units, which could travel at eighty-three miles an hour. To

Placing two locomotives at the head of a train was called double-heading. Each required an engineer and fireman and the practice was only justified when there was enough tonnage on the train to make both locomotives work hard. The locomotives here are Northerns, the lead one 6244 built in 1943. The train is heading east at the foot of Strachan Avenue in Toronto in May 1955. (J.V. Salmon photo, Metropolitan Toronto Reference Library)

The Continental Limited is eastbound in the Athabasca Valley passing Windy Point in the 1940s. The train is pulled by a 6000 series Mountain type, introduced into CN service in 1925.

A steamy Northern No. 6100 makes a winter afternoon start out of Halifax with *The Maritime Express* on its 840-mile, twenty-seven hour journey to Montreal. This was the oldest CN "name train," inaugurated in 1898 by the Intercolonial Railway two decades before its assets were taken over by CN.

A three-car electric train on the Mount Royal tunnel route from downtown Montreal. The tunnel, the longest in the country after the CPR tunnels in the Rockies, was dug by Canadian Northern just before World War I through three miles of volcanic rock.

French version of the logo egan to appear in print naterials in the early 950s.

assure daily departures from both east and west, eight sets of two units each were needed. Because of shorter stops the streamlined "Super" cut half a day off the trip, and with sections from Montreal and Toronto consolidating at Capreol, Ontario, it often totalled twenty air-conditioned coaches, sleeping cars, lounge cars and diners, as well as express, mail and baggage cars. Dome cars, called Sceneramic Lounge cars, were added later for the run through the Rockies.

CN completed its switch to diesels on April 25, 1960, when a 4-8-2 Mountain type built in 1929, hauling train No. 76, made its final run south from The Pas to Winnipeg, the last steam locomotive in regular CN service. Splendid in white tires, and driven by engineer Len Routledge and fireman Nicholas Shewchuk, the steamer was draped at Winnipeg station with a banner, "Farewell to 6043 C.N.R's Last Steam Locomotive," and honoured by Premier Duff Roblin and 750 nostalgic officials, pensioners and rail buffs. J. R. McMillan, vice-president of the western region, spoke for all, lamenting the demise of "that thundering, glamorous giant of the road." The steam locomotives were sent to scrapyards, museums and public parks, though three Northerns, one Mountain and two Pacifics were kept for excursions.

The 1960s were years of innovation. In its first reorganization in thirty-seven

(Overleaf) Saskatoon was a busy railway point around the noon hour in 1953 as trains linking it with Winnipeg, Calgary, Edmonton and Melfort met to exchange passengers. Narrow-gauge tracks were used for supplying ice to air-conditioned cars and for equipment maintenance materials, leaving the platforms free for passengers, mail and express. At far right is the "house track" for business cars, the mobile offices cum living quarters used by officials for line inspection and other road trips.

Twenty-nine carloads of locomotive coal at Spadina Roundhouse, Toronto, in 1953. The forty tons in each car would fill four tenders with a day's supply. To the right is the conveyor carrying ashes from locomotive ashpans to waiting gondola cars for use as fill and surfacing.

Suburban tank engine 49 was, in August 1957, the last steam locomotive overhauled at Montreal's Point St. Charles shops. This 4-6-4T locomotive was designed for double-ended operation on the commuter trains between Montreal and nearby Vaudreuil. The small integral coal bunker and water tank gave the engineer a good view in either direction. The last steam shop on the system was Stratford, which turned out rebuilt steamers for two more years, then closed its doors. The Point St. Charles, Transcona and Moncton shops converted to diesel maintenance.

years CN created eighteen management areas, each with an unprecedented degree of autonomy. A new logo was unveiled, the letters CN in a single, flowing line, symbolizing the movement of people, materials and messages. Diesels were painted with diagonal black and white stripes and ruddy orange noses.

The CPR having given up on passengers, CN was virtually the only railway on the continent still interested in carrying people in the 1960s. In an effort to woo back those who had deserted the rails for highways and airways, CN modernized its image, renewing its aging passenger fleet and dressing service crews in new uniforms and its trains in a new paint scheme. It rewrote schedules, spent heavily on advertising and introduced incentive fares and modern equipment. In 1964 it added the streamlined *Champlain* from Montreal to Quebec City and a new transcontinental, the *Panorama*, to complement *The Super Continental*. The *Rapido*, in 1965 one of the fastest diesel trains on the continent, averaged sixty-

Before the automotive age, branch lines were vital to rural communities across the country. Forty-two-year-old locomotive 86 began life on the Grand Trunk and was still going strong on the forty-four-mile branch line between Lyn Junction near Brockville, Ontario, and Westport in 1952.

seven miles an hour and ran between Montreal and Toronto in four hours and fifty-nine minutes.

The 263 chefs, 330 waiters and 110 stewards on CN's ninety-three dining and twenty-seven café cars were encouraged to restore prewar standards. Speeding along at seventy miles an hour in a tiny, swaying, jolting stainless steel kitchen, chefs like Ronnie Robinson of the "Super" prepared an average of five hundred excellent dinners between Winnipeg and Vancouver. "Rear-end traffic" – sleeping cars, dining cars, parlour cars – was a loss leader, and Donald Gordon, complaining that people were the most demanding and least profitable of all railway business, described CN's passenger trains as "mobile hotels featuring Waldorf service at steakhouse prices."

"It was always first-class service," agreed dining car inspector Pat Bennett of Moncton. "The cooks used to bake their own pies on the train, huge roasts and twenty-five-pound turkeys. They had maybe a foot and a half clearance between

Locomotive 6212 powered *The Washingtonian* into the States and *The Montrealer* northbound, both overnight trains. The Northern locomotive is pictured during a night layover in 1955.

the stove and the cupboard. And hot? Those fellows must have lost twenty pounds a trip."

"It was wonderful, the meals they could turn out on those trains," said Albino Paolucci of Montreal, cook, waiter, dining car steward, sleeping car conductor and inspector during his forty-two year career. "A lot of people rode the train just because of the dining car, especially between Montreal and Toronto. We prepared meals from scratch. We had a big coal stove with two ovens and a grill on the side for broiling steaks, chops or fish and a steam table for vegetables. There were nine or ten employees in a dining car. We were like brothers working together because we lived together and travelled together, especially if you were assigned to a train for six months."

In 1968 CN began to experiment with the fast, sleek, though inadequately-tested *Turbo*, which could carry three hundred people in its seven cars. Powered by gas turbines, its streamlined aluminum body designed to cut wind resistance, the *Turbo* could clip an hour off the *Rapido*'s time between Montreal and Toronto when it was running properly at its average speed of eighty-four miles an hour.

"The *Turbo* was a great train with super brakes though it had been produced in a hurry and had to undergo changes to cope with cold weather," said engineer Robert C. Jones of Belleville, Ontario, who took the inaugural *Turbo* run. Jones,

(Facing page) A steam locomotive hauls trailers on the double track west from Toronto to Hamilton and London, Ontario, in 1956. CN had begun piggybacking trailers between Montreal and Toronto four years earlier. In the second photo, a Northern speeds east into Montreal in 1956 over the bridge where the Ottawa River joins the St Lawrence. The head-end cars carry priority merchandise and the rest of the train consists of piggyback trailers.

Circus elephants were the first down the ramps because they were needed to assemble the big top. The Ringling Brothers and Barnum & Bailey Combined Shows, whose train had just arrived in east-end Montreal in this 1955 photo, had a herd of fifty.

This 1955 Maple Leaf logo lasted only until the modern CN symbol was adopted six years later.

Trains that carried trailers piggyback between Montreal and Toronto, such as this one powered by three 1,750-horsepower General Motors units in 1959, usually ran overnight to suit city pickup and delivery schedules.

who had become a fireman in 1941 and ten years later an engineer on Northerns ("they were wonderful, ran like a watch") and other steamers, continued to pilot the *Turbo* until retirement in 1980. "By that time they were calling me Grandpa," he laughed.

With these enticements, passenger revenues doubled between 1962 and 1968, but then they began to decline. CN's experiment in courting passengers had undoubtedly been necessary in a crown corporation dedicated to serving its owners, the public, but in the long run the experiment supported the argument that Canada had too few people to support a profitable intercity railway passenger service in an age of automobiles and airplanes.

As D. B. Hanna, CN's first president, had predicted, CN's bread and butter must come from freight. Carrying record volumes of freight with less rolling stock than in the past, CN invested in equipment for a postwar economy in which large inventories had been replaced by "just in time" shipments. There had been a time when a forty-foot boxcar with a six-foot door was the industry standard, and as a virtual monopoly the railway had put an onus on the shipper to tailor merchandise to fit. Now, with fierce competition from the trucking industry, railways had to become more adaptable to customer needs. They began to transform themselves from retail carriers to specialists in containers and bulk commodities.

As computers replaced old-fashioned accounting methods, thousands of clerical staff lost their jobs. New signalling systems and the extension of Centralized Traffic Control closed hundreds of train order offices in stations across the country. The piggybacking of highway trailers on flatcars, which had begun in the 1950s between Montreal and Toronto, was extended across the country and

(Facing page) In 1955 the *Ocean Limited,* inaugurated between Montreal and Halifax in 1904, poses on Beloeil Bridge on the Richelieu River, thirty miles east of Montreal. White flag on the new 6500 series locomotive usually announced an "extra," but in this case heralded a special run for the photographer.

The Super Continental was introduced in 1955 to supplement *The Continental Limited.* "The Super" covered the 2,930 miles between Montreal and Vancouver in seventy hours with a consist of up to twenty cars, including the "Sceneramic" dome car shown in midtrain near Jasper, Alberta, in 1965.

was the first stage of the present-day intermodal traffic in which freight is carried in a big metal box that can be transferred from road to rail and back again. In its pursuit of freight, CN now had 8,500 miles of double track and became a North American leader in the technology of concrete ties and the continuous welded rail that gave trains a smoother ride and the roadbed a longer life.

As an arm of government, CN advanced Canada's northern frontier, opening 700 miles of new track to regions whose names stud the history of postwar expansion. Between 1950 and 1970 CN built seventeen lines into the north. From Hillsport, Ontario, it pushed tracks to the copper-mining town of Manitouwadge. It built north from Chibougamau, Quebec, to the copper and zinc mines around Lake Metagami, four hundred miles north of Ottawa, and from Beattyville, Quebec, to the zinc-producing region near Amos. In northern Manitoba it built the Lynn Lake line to carry nickel, copper and cobalt. In British Columbia, CN tracks were pushed through the Coastal Mountains to the Aluminum Company of Canada plant at Kitimat. CN also completed the Alberta Resources Rail-

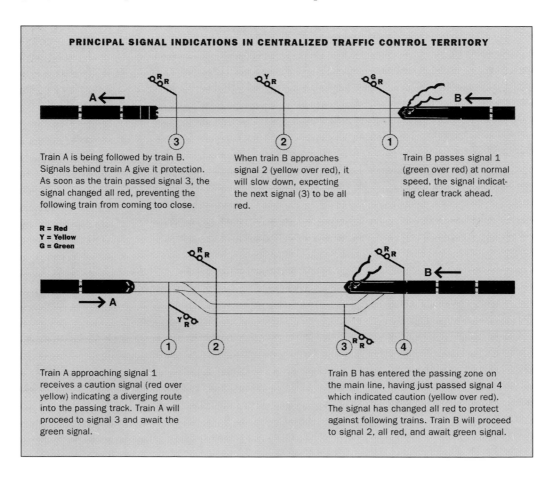

PRINCIPAL SIGNAL INDICATIONS IN CENTRALIZED TRAFFIC CONTROL TERRITORY

③ Train A is being followed by train B. Signals behind train A give it protection. As soon as the train passed signal 3, the signal changed all red, preventing the following train from coming too close.

② When train B approaches signal 2 (yellow over red), it will slow down, expecting the next signal (3) to be all red.

① Train B passes signal 1 (green over red) at normal speed, the signal indicating clear track ahead.

R = Red
Y = Yellow
G = Green

Train A approaching signal 1 receives a caution signal (red over yellow) indicating a diverging route into the passing track. Train A will proceed to signal 3 and await the green signal.

Train B has entered the passing zone on the main line, having just passed signal 4 which indicated caution (yellow over red). The signal has changed all red to protect against following trains. Train B will proceed to signal 2, all red, and await green signal.

way in the foothills of the Rockies. The most spectacular project was the 377-mile northern railway to Pine Point on Great Slave Lake to serve Cominco's lead-zinc mine.

Having said good-bye to steam, by the late 1960s CN was operating two thousand diesel units, which increased the size of trains and changed operating procedures, maintenance and labour relations. Diesels also changed the look of the railways themselves, eliminating hundreds of water towers, coal docks, ash pits and the great mountains of coal stored across the country.

Since diesels did not require the firemen who traditionally had been the source of engineers, CN took the occasion to open the country's only diesel school with a simulator called Oscar, at Gimli, Manitoba. "The whole thing changed when the diesels came in," said Larry Steeves of New Glasgow, Nova Scotia, a telegrapher and station master who joined CN in 1939. "The whole railway changed. Diesels and computers together changed railroading."

The *Turbo* on a pre-inaugural test run from Montreal to Cornwall. It began regular service in 1968, a year after it was scheduled to appear during Canada's centennial year celebrations.

4

RAILWAY PEOPLE

LIKE SEAFARERS AND SOLDIERS, NINETEENTH-CENTURY RAILROADERS developed a unique culture to cope with a hard and hazardous trade. Sons followed fathers into an industry that promised a lifetime job and a chance of mobility and advancement.

As the biggest, most visible industry in the country the railway was all-pervasive. Railroading carried status, which CN celebrated with the *Canadian National March*, played by its own bands. There were towns where a conductor, an engineer and a station agent ranked close to the mayor and the doctor. Many were members of fraternal lodges, such as the Masons.

Born as they were in the Victorian era, railways emphasized the paternalistic as well as the hierarchical. They organized special trains for company picnics, supported sports teams, and contributed to such organizations as the Railway YMCAs, which offered railroaders lodging, recreation and study, and Frontier College, which provided adult education. Railways gave out travel passes and other employee perquisites. In return they insisted on discipline and devotion to duty and expected respect for seniority, which in any case was insisted on by the unions.

Cautioned to be "neat in appearance, courteous and orderly," operational staff were rewarded or punished with "brownie points." Under the Brown System of Discipline, originally devised by G.R. Brown for the New York Central, employees were occasionally awarded points for exceptional merit. More often, de-

At St. Albans on the Central Vermont Railway, boilermakers manhandle superheater pipes out of a Mikado in 1952. The superheater gave steam a second pass through the firetubes before it went on to the cylinders for expansion against the pistons.

Engineer Cain "oiling around" a Pacific type locomotive in 1934, preparing to leave Moncton for Saint John, a three-hour trip with thirty-two stops. Conductor Clark holds a clearance form conveying authority to move onto the main line.

merit ranging from loss of a day's pay to dismissal was the penalty for failure to abide by the rules.

The "railway bible" was the red-bound, 163-page booklet *The Uniform Code of Operating Rules*, which employees had to learn like a catechism and keep with them on the job. A flawless timepiece was the "railway deity" and everyone in the "running trades" – numbering perhaps thirteen thousand people at any one time – was ordered to buy a standard railway watch, which had to be kept within a variation of thirty seconds a week and checked biweekly by one of two hundred watch inspectors. Before starting a run, conductor and engineer ceremoniously checked their watches, one against the other.

As boss of the train, the conductor has been compared with the master of a merchant ship, but there were significant differences. The captain on his bridge could see where he was going; the conductor had to share responsibility for piloting the train with the engineer.

"The engineer's authority ended at the engine's draw bar," explained Mel Humble, a conductor from Sarnia, Ontario. "He looked after the engine. The rest was our responsibility, but when anything went wrong, who catches hell?" When all else failed – when the engine seemed set to roll past a point where orders called for a halt – the conductor back in the train could open a valve and bleed pressure from the air-brake system to bring the train to an emergency stop.

"One thing that sometimes happened, an engine would run out of water and you'd have to drain her and dump your fire so it didn't blow up," said R.J. Proulx, a vice-president of the United Transportation Union in Ottawa. He recalled

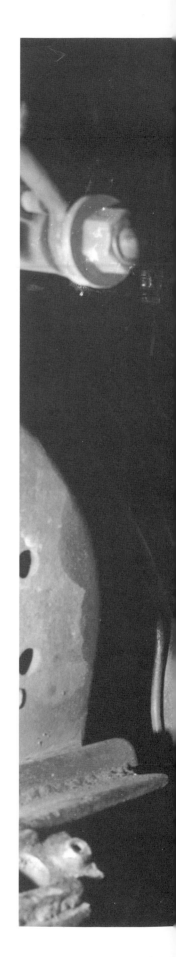

"Green all the way." A locomotive engineer pulls the throttle along a notched quadrant to control steam pressure to the cylinders. To the left of his throttle are steam- and air-pressure gauges and below his arm are brass brake handles, one for the locomotive, one for the train. When attached to a train, the locomotive was normally stopped by the drag of the train's braking system. Stuffed into crannies around the valves are wads of cotton waste, used copiously by the railways as wipers.

CONFEDERATION

27834

Engineer Duncan Campbell and fireman Robert McKay on the new Northern 6100 on its way to the Fair of the Iron Horse at Baltimore. For Canada's sixtieth anniversary in 1927 it was dubbed "Confederation."

that when he was serving as brakeman-conductor on a work train building the Chibougamau branch from Senneterre, Quebec, in 1959 the engine broke down completely and he had to walk twenty-five miles to get another.

Ordinarily, when a train had to stop out on the line, a brakeman would walk half a mile to show a red flag by day and lantern by night. His emergency kit included fusees, or flares, and track torpedoes, small explosive charges that were clipped on the rail and exploded under the wheels of a locomotive to warn the crew of danger. "I know one young brakeman who was out there too long and froze his foot and it had to be amputated," said Proulx. "When you got out there at night in winter the cold was so bad you had to be careful because you were inclined to go to sleep." In emergencies a train crew could communicate with dispatchers by attaching a portable phone to two of the CN telegraph and phone wires that ran on the poles along a right-of-way.

Before they were rendered redundant by diesel engines, brakemen outnumbered others of the operating crew. Freights carried a conductor and brakeman in the caboose and a second brakeman in the cab with the engineer and fireman. "You sat up by the boiler," said J. D. Cryon, thirty-nine years a brakeman and conductor. "In winter you burned on one side and were cold on the other. One time we were going down a hill heading for Brockville at three o'clock in the morning and the drive rod on the side of the engine broke. The rod would hit the ties and I thought we were going to turn over. The fire came out of the firebox and drove us back against the wall of the cab. We went three or four miles and tore everything up before we stopped." As in many other aspects of railroading, practices varied from region to region and in the West a third brakeman was carried on the longer trains.

Until recent years railroading demanded a great deal of muscle. A brakeman had to leap off a train and run like a deer to set the next switch. Before the automatic hump yards of the 1960s, in which cars were slowed by mechanical retarders operated from a control tower, a brakeman often rode a car as it was bunted forward by a switch engine and tended its hand brake until the car reached the proper track and train.

"It was worse in the winter with twenty-five pounds of clothing on your back and working around icy steel," said Cliff McCammon. From midnight to eight o'clock, McCammon's job was to ride a boxcar, jump off and run to throw a switch, jump back on the moving car and climb to the top to screw down the hand brake. "Some are lucky and some aren't," said McCammon, recalling the hazards

A brakeman repacks a journal box with oil-soaked cotton waste in 1947. If it dried out, the journal would overheat and burn, possibly destroying an axle and causing a derailment. Before roller bearings were introduced, the caboose crew were alerted to trouble by the pungent smell of a hot bearing.

In 1951 Everett Byers gives the highball for *The Continental Limited* to proceed through British Columbia. Though Byers signals by swinging his arm by day and a lantern by night, the term derives from the old ball signal hauled up a pole when the track was clear.

Called out by steam whistle, a brakeman atop a swaying boxcar uses a hardwood pole to screw down the brake wheels one by one. A modern train can be halted by air brakes, applied, as a fail-safe measure, not by an increase of air pressure but by a decrease.

of stepping into the path of an engine or a boxcar running loose. At the Saskatoon switchyard after World War II, McCammon was one of eighteen three-man crews, each with its switch engine, engineer and fireman and ninety cars to shunt in a night.

Once past examinations in signals, brakes, timetables and operating rules, the brakeman became eligible to become a conductor, responsible for the train arriving safely and on time without exceeding speed limits. A freight conductor wore overalls, sometimes a neckerchief to keep cinders out of his shirt, and his trouser bottoms tied tight so they would not catch. He did the accounts and time sheets and knew the contents and destination of each car and saw that they were detached or picked up properly.

Railroaders far from home lived in bunkhouses and cabooses or the Railway YMCA, introduced from the States in 1896 to provide cheap accommodation, reading rooms, and religious, educational and recreational activities. The first Railway Y was in Toronto; by the 1920s there were twelve at various division points such as Capreol and Sioux Lookout.

The freight conductor and brakemen, like the turtle, travelled with their own home. Redolent of tobacco smoke and lamp oil, the caboose was a cosy retreat when wind and snow beat on the storm windows. From his command post in the cupola the conductor could watch the entire train. Until it was replaced in recent years by the automated Train Information Braking System (TIBS), every freight had its tail-end caboose, with marker lamps red at the rear and green at front and sides. Introduced in the 1860s, the caboose was office, bedroom and kitchen, its odd name derived from *kabuse*, a German term for a ship's cookhouse. Steel cabooses with spring-loaded couplers that absorbed the jolting were a welcome improvement on the old types. "A tramp caboose could be pretty rough because no one cared," said Cryon, "but if you had your own, you took care of it. Some of the boys had linoleum on the floor and curtains on the windows. Sometimes the brakeman or conductor would be a good cook and do a roast. On the old type of caboose the coal stove was bolted to the floor, and I remember the jarring was so bad a stove lifted right up off the floor."

Passenger locomotives were built for speed, freight engines for power and traction. A way freight might average twelve miles an hour in the course of a day,

Hand brakes were used in yard operations long after the introduction of air brakes on the main line. Brakemen riding boxcars, shunted to roll onto the proper track, brought them to a halt by screwing down the brake wheels.

and the conductor of a meandering freight worked longer hours than the conductor of a closely scheduled passenger train. An unscheduled "extra" might find itself in and out of sidings half a dozen times on a run of 120 miles and have a dozen train orders – restricting speeds at level crossings and bridges, ordering "meets" with opposing trains and warning where it must give way to following trains with greater priority.

Railroaders in the running trades worked so much mileage per month. If they clocked up their quota in less than a month, they booked off until their prescribed month was up and then started again. To alleviate the loneliness, the wives of men away for days and weeks at a time joined church or union auxiliaries, bridge clubs and quilting circles and devised collective child care. Nan Shepley of Winnipeg, wife of a CN locomotive engineer, lived in a boxcar at Graham, a little community between Thunder Bay and Sioux Lookout, between 1926 and 1928. The perils included the occasional incursions of drunken bushmen. Two trappers came into town one day, crazy drunk on homebrew, shot up the railway station, shot out the lights at a dance in the school and killed a man who was shaving in the railway bunkhouse. One of the trappers killed the other before he was tackled and subdued by a seventeen-year-old apprentice brakeman. "We cut down the station agent's clothesline to truss up the criminal," Nan Shepley recalled.

For railway wives, irregular hours were a way of life. Jean Humble of Sarnia said that her husband, Mel, might go to work at one o'clock in the afternoon, or at eight o'clock in the morning or at midnight. "It was your life. You had to do it. When he went on a freight there was a complete change of clothes every time he came in. Overalls and smocks and things to wash. There was a lot of laundry. Not much social life."

"You worked the craziest hours," recalled J. D. Cryon. "You lived by the telephone and went to work when they called you. You couldn't make any plans. You were away at Christmas and New Year's more often than you were at home. You never

To protect the rear of a train making an unscheduled stop, a trainman walked back a thousand yards with a red flag or lantern and a flagging kit that contained fusees, matches and track torpedoes to warn an approaching engine. This trainman carries lantern and red fusee.

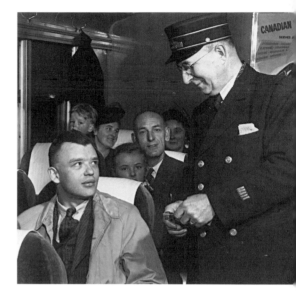

Chief of operations, chief accountant, keeper of the peace and font of information, the conductor was the symbol of authority on a passenger train. Normal practice was to seat passengers according to destination to simplify the task of ticket collecting.

A freight conductor (right) keeps watch from his observation post in the cupola of a caboose on a run from Montreal to Winnipeg in 1947. The earliest cabooses were boxcars with windows, no cupola and very little comfort. (Below) In caboose 77052 of a Grand Trunk Western freight in 1946, a conductor works at the desk under a set of ornate oil lamps in his mobile office and home while the rear-end brakeman watches the right-of-way.

A freight conductor and brakeman fork up sausages and beans on chipped enamel plates, standard issue aboard a caboose. In this 1954 photo there are oil lamps on the wall and a "Quebec heater" in the corner.

knew what was going to happen when you went out to work. I packed a pretty big bucket for food, always four or five meals. Carried it in a club bag. Unless you worked on a passenger train the wife never knew when to expect you home."

On passenger trains the conductor and brakemen, who were called trainmen, wore dark blue uniforms, white shirts, well polished shoes, brass or silver buttons, and service bars. The company's most visible representatives, many were naturally avuncular and good-natured as they worked their way down the lurching aisle collecting tickets, calling out the stations, ensuring that people got off at the proper stops, calling "All aboard!" and keeping order. Most answered passengers' questions with patience, but some grizzled veterans of long years of hard braking on freights were undeniably crusty.

The long, hard apprenticeship required before a brakeman became a passenger conductor was poor training in public relations. The brakeman was out in all weathers in a hazardous job with few social niceties. "It's dangerous on a train if you don't watch yourself," said Bill Cronin of Sarnia, twenty years a brakeman

and fifteen a conductor. "I preferred passenger trains. You met more people. They looked up to you because you were the boss and had a uniform."

"Braking was dangerous in those days," agreed his friend Bill Schram, a brakeman for twenty years before promotion to conductor during World War II. "The equipment was not like it is today."

"Maybe one cold winter night your train would break in two," recalled J. D. Cryon. "Freight trains are like roller coasters. Early on they never had the sliding equipment that gives with the pull of a train. You might have an eighty-car train and you'd run down a grade and then start up another and the slack might break a weak knuckle, the coupler that holds two cars together. The darn thing would never break near the engine or near the caboose but always halfway up the train, and you'd have to carry a knuckle. They weighed about seventy-five pounds, and they had a hole on the end. You'd shove a broomstick through the thing and throw it over your shoulder. You'd walk through the snow to lug this thing up to the break in the train. Before they got radios and walkie-talkies, which were terrific, we would light fusees so the engineer could see back in darkness or fog."

Dispatchers gave a copy of train orders to both conductor and engineer, who read the tissue-thin "flimsies" together. "All you had to do was make one mistake and that could cost you dearly," said engineer Alex Douglas of Thunder Bay. "So you always double-checked the train orders."

The engineer in bibbed overalls, brass buttons, striped, high-crowned peak cap, goggles and neckerchief was a trained craftsman. The source of his nickname "hogger" or "hoghead" is obscure but it may have originated in the U.S.

Sorting mail under a Pintsch gas lamp (facing page) while the train sped through the night in 1937. The first mail car in Canada was introduced by the Grand Trunk in 1855. Post office cars operated between key Canadian cities in fast passenger trains, and all through the trip postal employees sorted mail for distribution at destination. Mobile sorting continued until airlines began to carry mail on a large scale after World War II.

Handling mail at Winnipeg. Most mail moved in head-end cars on passenger trains. Baggage wagons piled high with sacks were trundled into position ready for the train to come in.

with the big 2-8-0 Consolidations, called hogs because of their greedy consumption of water for making steam. The engineer worked irregular, often nocturnal shifts. He had to know the tonnage of his loaded train, the location of bridges and level crossings, where sidings were and how many cars they would hold. He had to know speed limits as he guided his heavy train around curves and uphill and down, and since there were no speedometers on the steamers he clocked himself by the mile boards along the right-of-way, forty-four to the mile. With a diesel he had a speedometer.

"Years ago," said engineer Frank Fagan of Moncton, "an engineer had a locomotive assigned to him and he hated to lose that engine. Took pride in it. On a way freight you had a lot of time to polish and keep it clean. But all that disappeared with World War II. I liked the Northern 6200s the best of any of them. They were passenger engines and nice to run. Freight engines in this area were usually Mikados, and the 6100 Northerns and the Santa Fe 4000s were powerful engines, hauling big coal trains. With diesels, the wheels were all underneath, but you take a nice high-wheeler steam engine like a 6100 or 6200 with white rims on them and the black background – they looked nice and neat. I never had much use for diesel power, although I've got to admit it was a much easier, cleaner job. I was a steam man. There was something there that seemed to be a living thing. I could put up with a little bit of coal dust and the odd cinder in my eye. If you had a good head of steam you could get over the road much better than you could with a diesel, as far as I'm concerned."

Because intense cold stiffened and cracked air-brake hoses and shrank the gaskets between them, a fifty-car train in summer might well be a twenty-five-car train in winter. "You couldn't go with more than a five-pound leakage," said Alex Douglas of Thunder Bay. "If the leakage was great enough, we'd stop and pump the train up and make a test and if there was a

Steam locomotives demanded great quantities of water every fifty miles or so. No. 7516, whose tender holds 6,000 gallons, is taking on water before starting work switching freight cars at Turcot Yard, Montreal.

The switch just in front of this shiny Northern type No. 6258 is set for the track at the left of the steep incline to the coal bunker. The bunker was serviced by six-wheel yard switchers hauling hopper cars of coal. (J. Norman Lowe photo)

A star of CN's war effort, a big Northern type No. 6180 built in 1940, is coaled with a clamshell crane while a mechanic's pressure gun forces Alemite grease into the bearings of the running gear. (J. Norman Lowe photo)

ten- or twelve-pound leakage we'd have to set off cars on the side tracks and re-duce the size of the train if we couldn't repair the leak. Leave them there until warmer weather. You started out with eighty or ninety cars and maybe got to Atikokan with sixty. It would be thirty below zero."

George Harrison, firing out of Portage la Prairie, Manitoba, recalled a prairie night so cold – forty below zero with a wind – that the engine froze to the tracks before the operation of taking on water could be completed. Once it got free, snowdrifts were so high, obstructing the view, that the engine ran into the caboose of a snowplow that had been trying to clear the way ahead. "We were obliged to stay there all night in that predicament. Our passengers on train No. 1 were splendid. Our engine was dead and they came out of the carriages and shovelled snow for four hours to fill the tender with water to get us going. We were delayed twenty-four hours."

Frozen switches and signals increased the danger of collision. Though it took a lot of snowflakes to put a 250-ton engine into the ditch, blizzards were known to strand whole trains. "I've seen drifts twelve, fourteen feet deep," recalled Frank Fagan.

Winter in the Rockies, 1953. It took two locomotives to propel this wedge plow through a snow-filled rock cut. Rotary plows, invented in Canada, were also used.

Frank Keefe of Winnipeg, who rose from call boy through telegraph operator, dispatcher and superintendent to western general manager, said the chief emergencies of his time were in the Rockies – rock slides, mud slides, snow slides, washouts, derailments and equipment failures. In the winter of 1949–50 forty snow slides west of Kamloops held up service for three weeks. One train, carrying sixty transcontinental passengers, was hit by a slide that broke the windows in the dining and observation cars, filled them with snow and threatened to topple the cars into the river. "We walked the passengers to a CN work camp. We had men make paths across the slides, with one man to each passenger to take them across. There they got blankets, mattresses, etc., and the dining car crew cooked and served food there." The train was stuck for several days before rotary plows sent by dispatcher Bruce Davis at Kamloops could dig it out. "The Fraser Canyon is a horrible piece of country even when the weather is good," Keefe said. "We were just snowed in there. It was terrible."

Jack Cann recalled his service as a maintenance engineer in the five hundred-mile Kamloops Division. "I had more draglines, more shovels, more bulldozers working in the Kamloops division than the rest of CN system put together. In six

(Right) Soot, grease, oil and dust combined with water vapour from condensed steam to form a grey-brown film on a locomotive, which the roundhouse staff would periodically scrub off. (J. Norman Lowe photo)

months we pulled thirteen engines out of the canyon. These were partly caused by washouts, partly by slides. February and November were bad times. We had superb wrecking crews. They had lots of practice."

"Snowplows, that was something again," said Joe Cernak of Calgary, who once fired the locomotive of a plow for twenty-four hours straight. "Because of the heat in the cab, water from the snow would be running through all the holes and cracks. It would be twenty-five below outside, but we'd be sweating in oil-skins and trying to shovel coal. We'd be soaked, and men outside would have to serve us for coal and water because we couldn't go outside where we'd freeze to death. So this water would be flying down on us. What a mess. You'd run into cold snow and would have to back up and ram at it and force your way through, back up, and finally break a hole through it and keep on going."

"It was strictly on-job training," said engineer Graham Crossman of Saskatoon, whose apprenticeship lasted eleven years. A fireman, who must have good health, eyesight and grade school literacy, endured a long apprenticeship before he gained the engineer's seat on the right side of the cab.

"I started on the end of a shovel and ended up running a fast freight to Edmundston, New Brunswick," said Frank Fagan. "The pay was better on a freight." Fagan was an engineer for most of his thirty-six years at CN, but he didn't mind firing when there was good coal to work with. "That was the big thing – good coal – but it wasn't too easy a job, especially on a hot day with eighty-five degrees."

As the train rattled along at sixty miles an hour or more with steam gauge at 275 pounds, the foot-plate jigging and steam hissing, the fireman not only kept an eye on the gauges but watched from the left side of the cab and noted the warnings on order boards as the train sped past stations.

Teamwork was essential. If the engineer mishandled his valve cutoff and failed to create a proper draft for the firebox, the fireman would fight a losing battle to keep a head of steam. "You were as good as

(Below) No. 5700, one of the Hudson types introduced to compete with the CPR's stable of these famous locomotives, was mostly seen on the main line between Montreal and Toronto or in southwest Ontario. Here, in the early 1950s, it is about to leave Ottawa's Union Station, now the Conference Centre, across the street from the Chateau Laurier, one of CN's most famous hotels before it was sold. (J. Norman Lowe photo)

Northern type 6205 on the hundred-foot turntable at Turcot Roundhouse during World War II. The roundhouse was established in 1905 by the Grand Trunk Railway and closed down in 1961. As many as 145 locomotives a day could be served at its fifty-six stalls.

the engineer you worked with," said Crossman. "I had a lot of good ones, but there were cantankerous engineers it was impossible for trainees to work with."

"If the engineer didn't like you," said Joe Cernak, "you kept to your side of the cab. They called us 'tallowpots' because of our long-spouted oilcan with thick, greenish tallow oil for the cylinders. When the engineer was mad at you, he could slip the drive wheels when starting out and 'pull your fire' so you'd have to get the long hook and pull your fire back so you didn't have it piled up in spots on the grates. Once the grates were uncovered you'd lose steam. Some of those engineers were real mean. They would do this on purpose if they thought you were a hotshot fireman, which we all thought we were. They would try to suck us down into submission. It was a clash of personalities."

William Law had been a switchman for forty-four years when this photograph was taken in 1927. He had lost an arm but not his job.

The poor combustion that produced telltale black smoke was not always the fault of fireman or engineer. In the 1950s when CN converted to diesels, it insisted on using up the coal that had been stored for decades in great piles half a mile long and a hundred feet high. "It had dirt and stones and trees growing through it," said Graham Crossman. "You didn't go far until you stalled, on account of the clay and stuff in that coal. It was just terrible. You had two sorts of locomotives. The larger type was equipped with a mechanical stoker, but you still had a lot of the smaller engines which were hand-fired with the old scoop shovel. It was hard work."

"I've seen firemen no bigger than five foot two, weighing maybe 135 pounds dripping wet," said Jim Munsey, "and they'd fire an engine up, take maybe eight or nine hours getting there, and they'd have a cup of coffee and come back and do the same thing over again."

"The first thing a fireman would do after you stowed your lunch pail and coat away," said Lorne Brisbin, "was to check your firebox to see there were no bad leaks and there was oil in the lubricators, and then you'd climb on the tender to make sure you had a full tank of water and full hopper of coal.

"You'd put in a fire, get a cup of water, sit down a minute or maybe eat half a sandwich. You had your steam gauge. When it was ascending you didn't need any more coal. You needed a nice, white, bright fire. Incandescent almost. When it started to die down a bit it would get red. When your fire started to get oily and dirty-looking, you were firing too heavily. To control the level of water, which had to be more or less constant in the boiler, you had your water glass.

"Steam was more of an art than diesel. The main valve that allowed steam into the superheater units was controlled by a big throttle that took a bit of energy to haul out or close. Some engineers were real artists and could run over the road and use less coal and keep a swing on the train while others just wouldn't use the right valve cutoff and throttle setting and the engine would be almost choking itself."

Though the conductor and engineer ran the train, their movements were orchestrated by the dispatcher in a distant command post. Minutes and seconds were his métier, and the train-sheet the ledger in which he balanced one train against another and assured a safe flow of traffic. Before radio communication arrived, telegraph operators, who might also be station agents and jacks-of-all-trades, were his eyes and ears. They kept the dispatcher informed as each train passed their station and warned of such danger signs as a "hotbox" – an overheated journal or bearing.

Dispatchers at the centre of a busy web of tracks had one of the most stressful jobs in railroading. Alfred Bureaux, a dispatcher at Moncton, recalled one winter day when he had to juggle two passenger trains, three freight trains and three snowplows that were all running slow. "I've seen days I would put seventy or eighty train orders out, and that's a lot of work. I've seen days I brought my lunch home because I didn't have time to eat it."

"You had the rule book and the time card," said Bruce Davis, who retired as dispatcher at Kamloops in 1960. "Passenger trains are usually first-class trains

A bed of coals is visible through the firebox door as the fireman adds a scoop of coal. Before CN became the first railway in Canada to introduce the automatic stoker, it was the fireman's job to keep the big square grate evenly covered with coal for maximum heat, shifting perhaps two tons an hour at 133 shovelfuls per ton.

With a chief dispatcher at his shoulder, a divisional dispatcher pores over a 1940s train-sheet on which he has logged everything that moved over his hundred miles of track during an eight-hour shift. Dispatchers controlled "meets" on single track, transmitting orders to station operators, who passed them on to train crews.

Operator E. J. Saulnier receives a train order by dispatcher's telephone at Halifax in 1939 and makes copies on flimsy paper interleaved with carbons. To the right of his head are the telegraph sounder and levers controlling train order signals.

and speed freights are second class trains and there are others, the extras and so on. Then your eastbound trains are superior to westbound trains of the same class and these things are all mixed up in there and you have to keep everybody sorted out and moving."

Once an engine was under way, changes in train orders were telegraphed to the next station, where they were stuck in a hooped stick which a crewman snatched on the fly. "We ordered up the trains," said Jim Munsey of Edmonton, who became a dispatcher at the unusually young age of twenty-one. "We controlled them en route, told them where to meet and where to wait, which trains to pass and which not to pass. Try to keep them from hitting one another on the road. It was all interlocked. You tried to set it up so they met with a minimum of delay and no risk of collision."

Bureaux remembered a head-on collision near Antigonish, Nova Scotia, in which an engineer forgot there was to be a "meet" of freight trains from east and west. Three men were killed. But human failures were not always to blame. Near Bathurst, New Brunswick, one March morning, Bureaux got a call warning that a thirty-car ore train was out of control on a branch line with only the engineer aboard.

"The driver came on his radio and said, 'I'm going by Brunswick Mills and she's doing fifty-five miles an hour and I can't hold her.' He kept talking to me off and on and finally I said, 'Is there any way you can get off that damn thing? Can you bail out into a snowbank or something?' But he said, 'No I can't, Alf. I've got to stay with it.' One of the reasons he stayed, and the man deserves a lot of credit, there were three or four railroad crossings geared for trains going twenty miles an hour. But by now he was doing seventy-two and it was quarter after eight in the morning and school buses out on the highways. He stayed with the train, just for that reason, blowing the whistle for crossings. The sad part, there's nothing you can do about a runaway train except warn people to stand back. I

Train orders were picked up by head-end cab crews from long-handled hoops as a train steamed by. At Turcot marshalling yard, Montreal, in 1950, an operator holds an order hoop about to be snatched by the crew of locomotive 3727.

Tracks serving Montreal's Bonaventure Station were controlled at the Mountain Street Tower. In this 1936 photo the operator takes instructions from a dispatcher while the lever man prepares to work the rods and cranks attached to a distant switch, which might be half a mile away.

Typical of the pre-computer age, the Machine Bureau of the Auditor of Accounts in Winnipeg depended on "the Machine," a Comptometer, which was essentially a speedy adding machine.

got hold of Bathurst and said, 'Get the ambulance, the fire department, doctor, and get up to Nepisiguit as fast as you can.' We expected the worst." The runaway train reached Nepisiguit, where the branch entered the main line, and though the main line was clear there was no time to switch through and the train crashed off the tracks. Because snow flooded the cab and cocooned him, the engineer escaped death.

In a larger junction where tracks converged, a man in a tower stood ready to pull levers, throw switches, set rails and reroute trains. "He'd be sitting there reading a book, drinking coffee, and then all hell would break loose," said Jim

Munsey. "There'd suddenly be trains coming from every direction and everyone wanting to get through. The dispatcher would set priorities, which one he'd take first. If he made a mistake, he might expose a train to a tail-end collision. You really had to use your head."

"Back in the days before radio communication, when you delivered orders to a station for a train on the line, and it passed that station, it was gone until the next station," said Jim Munsey. "If you made a mistake, there was no way you could get hold of him to tell him to stop. He was headed for disaster. One dispatcher missed a train order and there was a head-on collision. He turned grey in

Craftsmen "quartering" the driving wheels of a locomotive in the shops at Transcona (from "Transcontinental") near Winnipeg in 1934. To assure a proper relationship with the thrust of the pistons, the wheels on each axle were offset by a very precise quarter turn.

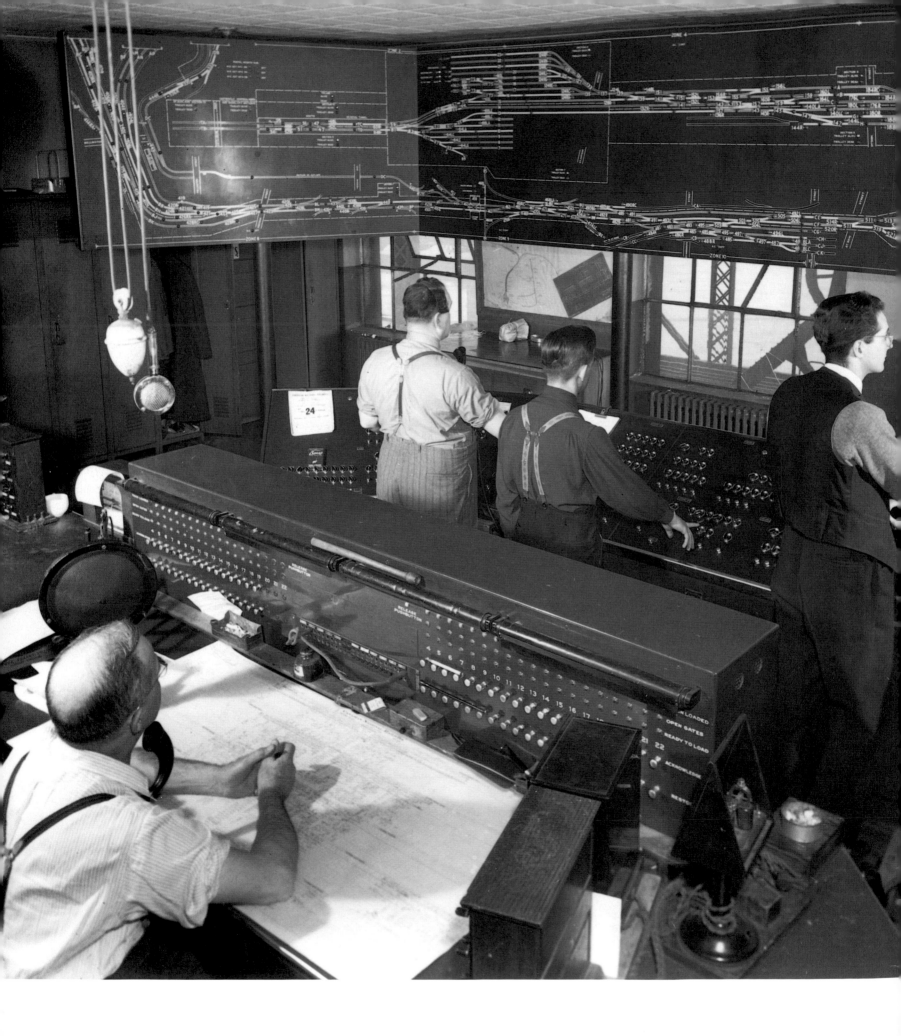

a matter of days. I remember another chap here in Edmonton who discovered he had issued what we call a lap order, giving two trains the same authority on the same track at the same time. But it was on the prairie and they saw each other coming and stopped. Another dispatcher set up trains out of Jasper and forgot about one of them and in effect had a lap order, a big heavy westbound freight and a little way freight out of Jasper. They all jumped off. It was a terrible thing to live with if you were responsible for somebody being killed.

"I found it to my advantage to know every curve and grade, and to know every engineman, because they all had different personalities. Some were gamblers, some were cautious. So when the chips were down you could figure which guy would go and which would hang back. This guy will go, I know him, he'll take a chance. The other guy, he's too cautious, he won't go. You had to know your engines because some steamed better than others, and know who the fireman was — can this guy keep a heavy steam up? All this counted, and if you got out and rode with them on your days off you learned these things. There were some great guys who would drop into the beer parlour for a couple of beers on the turnaround, and they'd make 'black smoke,' as we called it, telling railway stories, how they did this or how that happened. You'd tuck all this away."

The running trades were represented by the international Big Four: the Brotherhood of Locomotive Firemen and Enginemen (BLF&E), Brotherhood of Locomotive Engineers (BLE), Order of Railway Conductors (ORC) and the Brotherhood of Railroad Trainmen (BRT). Then came the carmen, boilermakers and blacksmiths of Division No. 4 of the American Federation of Labor, and

A sleeping car porter returns a pair of freshly polished shoes to their owner's compartment cupboard via a little door from the aisle. The porter kept track of the owners by marking the soles with the compartment number.

Wellington Tower controlled trains around the Montreal terminal including Central Station (the tracks, top centre) and Turcot Yard (lower right). The controller at the raised desk has voice communication with staff all over the area, and the three men control switches and signals, their actions recorded in lights on the panel above, which show moving trains.

members of the Order of Railway Telegraphers and the Canadian Brotherhood of Railway Employees.

The blacks represented by the Order of Sleeping Car Porters occupied a special niche until the 1960s when other railway jobs began to open up for them. Leonard Dixon, who joined CN in Halifax in 1939 said, "As a person of colour, the only job you could apply for in CN was sleeping car porter. They made that quite clear. If you applied for a labourer's job, they would direct you to the sleeping car department. As far as I was concerned it was a good place to work. You were making more pay than a waiter and the waiters were all white. You had a pension plan. The majority of blacks that sent their kids to university were sleeping car porters."

A pecking order was a basic feature of railroading. A fireman from Barrie, Ontario, recalled attending a church service in a northern Ontario railway town during World War II where locomotive engineers refused to sit on the same side of the aisle as firemen. There was an even bigger gap in status between people in the elite running trades and other railway employees.

"One of our favourite sayings in those days," said Jim Munsey, a railroader all his life like his father, "was the difference between a 'railroader' and a 'man who worked for the railroad.' A railroader was always figuring ahead. When I hired out, my dad used to tell me that railroaders were the aristocrats of labour. You strived to build a reputation and had a great sense of satisfaction if you achieved everything required of you, to get a train safely through its run, because everything that happened was a co-operative effort between the crews, the dispatchers and operators and further down the line the condition of the track and equipment."

Jacques Gauthier of Montreal recalled that when he was a foreman at Taschereau in northern Quebec in 1949 his men worked around the clock in

In the kitchen of a dining car every bit of space was needed. Dry groceries such as cereal and flour were stacked above refrigerated lockers containing fish, meat and ice cream. Plates and pots were warmed above the coal-fired range in this 1933 photo.

inner in the diner was state f the art in the 1930s. ever was there better food, ervice and tableware, enanced by air conditioning to ilute the inevitable cigar nd cigarette smoke. This romotion shot employs the ame cast of CN staff memers as the photo of the arlour car on page 87.

The 1939 Royal Train carrying King George VI and Queen Elizabeth across Canada consisted of equipment from CN and the CPR, all of it painted royal blue and silver. The dining car and crew were supplied by CN.

twelve-hour shifts seven days a week. "We had sixty-five to seventy men, half of them carmen. Every thirty days a steam engine had to be washed out. You had to damp the fire, remove the plugs and wash the interiors, the hoses, the boiler, and make sure all accumulation of rust was taken out and the tubes cleaned of dust."

More than twelve thousand people in three thousand sections maintained CN's thirty thousand miles of steel, wood and crushed rock against the pounding of heavy trains and weather. "All of the boys were on call twenty-four hours a day . . . no shifts . . . to keep this section open to traffic," said Fred Rolfe, a section foreman at Halifax. While engineers might be the aristocrats, "they don't move without us." Most sectionmen were members of the Brotherhood of Maintenance of Way Employees and each year replaced track, worn ties and ballast. Five or six section foremen reported to a roadmaster, who ensured that tracks were properly maintained. Until welded rail eliminated the need to tighten joints, four section-men under a foreman patrolled about eight miles of track, warning of washouts, landslides and so on. On stormy nights they would be out at the switches, keeping them clear of ice and snow. More recently, a foreman and two sectionmen were responsible for thirty-five miles of track.

Due to computers and efforts to extend employment to women, a third of CN's labour force was female by the mid-1970s. Women had begun to move into traditionally male jobs, as diesel repair engineers, sleeping car porters, mechanics and machinists, train announcers, station agents, section workers, electricians, police officers, yard masters and dispatchers, though few as yet had entered management or the running trades.

Modern technology had replaced the muscle power of yesteryear, and whether out on the line or in the office, workers could no longer be could guaranteed lifetime jobs on the railway as they had when steam was king. In an age of diesels, computers, automation and highways, old-fashioned railroading was the country of the past.

A degree of "super-elevation" of the track compensates for the train's centrifugal force by permitting it to lean into a curve. The device straddling CN's Central Vermont track contains a spirit level to measure the difference in height between the two rails.

(Facing page) When diesels replaced steam locomotives, CN kept three Northerns, two Pacifics and a Mountain type for excursions. Northern 6153's axle bearings are inspected before a Canadian Railroad Historical Association jaunt from Montreal to Joliette, Quebec, in 1960.

A rebuilt diesel is lowered onto a track. Inaugurated by the Grand Trunk Railway in 1857, the Point St. Charles shops, Montreal, maintained locomotives and rolling stock. In addition, thirty-four steam locomotives were built here.

As hazardous as it gets. The accident rate in "Avalanche Alley" (the Ashcroft subdivision in the British Columbia mountains, from Kamloops to Boston Bar), where many a train got into trouble and some tipped into the river, was reduced by modern technology, train radio, and slide detectors to warn of falling rock.

5

RAILROADING IN THE SPACE AGE

No LONGER THE NATIONAL INSTITUTION IT WAS FOR HALF A CENTURY, CN has been hard pressed during the past two decades to adapt to a new role. Despite vast improvement in railway technology – diesel locomotives, computers, automation and specialized freight cars and containers – an increasing proportion of the freight once hauled by trains is carried by trucks.

By the early 1990s CN, like the CPR, had shrunk dramatically in the battle to survive. In Newfoundland and Prince Edward Island, as well as on many branch lines across the country, the battle had been lost and the train had been succeeded by trucks and buses. Trackage had been reduced from 31,000 miles to 18,000. A work force of 130,000 in 1950 had been reduced by two-thirds. CN had sold its hotels, commercial communications and ships, and what was left of the waning passenger service had been surrendered to the new crown corporation VIA Rail.

In hardly more than a generation there had been more changes in railroading than at any time since Confederation, and not all changes had been due simply to new technology. The equality of women in the workplace had opened job opportunities hardly dreamed of a generation earlier. Women were beginning to appear in senior management and more than a hundred women were working as brakemen or even driving engines, aided by the fact the technology in diesel cabs no longer demanded the strength required by steam engines. Francine Leclerc of Montreal, a descendant of the famous Quebec strongman Louis Cyr,

To dramatize its passenger deficit, in 1977 CN created a new division, VIA CN, with a distinctive blue and yellow colour scheme. The following year VIA Rail Canada became a separate crown corporation operating former CN and CPR passenger trains.

The familar CN symbol was developed in 1960 and began appearing in 1961. Designer Allan Fleming said it was a continuous line representing a route from origin to destination for the movement of people, materials and messages. Some have nicknamed it the snake or wiggly worm. The treatment is also applied to the symbols for the Central Vermont and the Grand Trunk.

was one of the first women in the cab and recalls heads turning when she drove a diesel from Montreal to the U.S. border. "I felt a bit like a special circus animal," she said. Starting as a brakeman, she had overcome resistance in company and union to gain the coveted engineer's seat. "There were a lot of reasons I wanted to do it," she said. "I liked the thrill of achievement. I didn't find it difficult. I'm physically strong, and driving a locomotive is more than anything a matter of judgement and memory."

In the hump yards of Montreal, Toronto, Winnipeg and Moncton automation had replaced the slow process in which engines banged and butted cars into position to form new trains. Traffic Reporting and Control System (TRACS) monitored CN's two thousand diesel locomotives and hundred thousand freight cars by means of trackside electronic scanners reading coded information stuck to the sides of rolling stock. CN's command centre in Montreal these days looks like the bridge of a starship. Operators keep an eye on trains across Canada by means of multicoloured schematics glowing on a giant screen.

Railways were safer and more efficient than at any time in their history, though there had been setbacks. The *Turbo* train, designed in the 1970s as an alternative to air travel between Montreal and Toronto, was a well-publicized disappointment. After years of mechanical troubles and excessive fuel costs, the revolutionary train powered by a turbine engine was replaced by the LRC (Light, Rapid, Comfortable), a compromise between the streamlined *Turbo* and the heavier trains of the past.

CN was one of the last railways on the continent to try to maintain passenger service. And even when the deficit from the "varnish service" had increased so much that CN joined the CPR in adopting a government plan to turn passengers over to VIA Rail Canada in 1978, CN continued to play a behind-the-scenes passenger role. It supplied VIA Rail with tracks and operating crews under a management contract, as well as supplying facilities for Amtrak, the U.S. passenger carrier, which reaches into Canada at Montreal and Toronto. In co-operation with the government of Ontario it operated the GO service designed to reduce

Francine Leclerc, her right hand on the brake lever, receives radio instructions at Taschereau Yard, Montreal, in 1994. Leclerc joined CN when opportunities in the running trades were opened to women in the early 1980s and worked up to the cab through apprenticeship as brakeman and conductor. She became one of CN's first female locomotive engineers in 1986 after training at CN's diesel school in Gimli, Manitoba. (Debbie Laramee photo)

In the 1930s the Royal York Hotel (left), towering over Union Station and four Pacific type locomotives, dominated the Toronto skyline. By 1993 (below) the hotel had been dwarfed by skyscrapers and the CN Tower. In the foreground is a GO Transit commuter train operated by CN under contract to the government of Ontario. (Lower photo: Jean B. Héguy)

the demand for new expressways around Toronto. In Quebec it contracted with the provincial government for commuter service at Montreal.

Otherwise, CN was free to concentrate on what it did best, hauling freight. Though it had traditionally made its profits from wholesale cargo like grain and coal, timber, ore and the products of heavy industry, it had also provided retail freight service, accepting the consignments of private individuals no matter how small or unprofitable. Now, having lost its monopoly, the railway no longer tried to be all things to all people. Light freight and branch-line services were gradually relinquished to the trucking industry. The old-fashioned mixed train that provided total freight and passenger service for hundreds of communities across the country disappeared.

Though CN still excelled at carrying bulk freight like grain, and two-thirds of the mining industry tonnage, container service had become the common denominator of modern transportation. Invented in the late 1950s for ocean shipping, containers had moved ashore by 1970 to begin replacing the piggybacking

In 1950 automobiles were loaded at the Ford plant in Windsor, Ontario, into boxcars with especially wide doors, four autos to a boxcar. By 1993 (below) autos were driven right onto a tri-level car, twice the length of the boxcars, that carried up to fifteen autos. (Lower photo: Jean B. Héguy)

(Facing page) In most cities valuable downtown railway land has been sold off for commercial development. In London, Ontario, (lower photo) CN's office tower looms beyond the station and a VIA Rail passenger train in 1993. The top photo, taken some fifty years earlier, shows three steam trains exchanging passengers for Toronto, Windsor and Goderich. (Lower photo: Jean B. Héguy)

of highway trailers, wheels and all, on railway flatcars. Having idle wheels piggy-backing on trains was not the most efficient use of transportation, so the next step had been aluminum containers, forty feet long and eight feet wide, which were loaded from warehouse or ship, carried across the country on flatcars, and taken to final destination by truck. In a service developed under the direction of Ronald E. Lawless, a career railroader who became CN's president in the 1980s, a "total intermodal system" began to account for an ever-larger proportion of the company's domestic freight tonnage and most of its overseas Atlantic traffic.

Specialized carriers had multiplied. In the past, CN had four basic freight cars, including the standard reddish-brown forty-foot boxcar, the flatcar for carrying timber and large machinery, and the open gondola and hopper car for coal, ore and other cargo that had to be top-loaded. By the 1980s freight cars for specific jobs became common. Covered cylindrical steel or aluminum hopper cars carried grain and potash. Pneumatic hoppers were equipped to discharge flowable cargo like sugar or flour into silos or highway trucks. There were rotary

In the top photo a double-headed freight, pulled by a Consolidation and a Mikado, steams off Montreal's Victoria Bridge in 1950 and into St. Lambert. Forty years later (below) a bypass around the St. Lambert lock of the St. Lawrence Seaway has changed the scene. As a CN intermodal train uses the by-pass, the old route is barely visible under the viaduct beyond the trees. (Lower photo: Jean B. Héguy)

gondolas that turned upside down for unloading, bi-level and tri-level auto-rack carriers laden with automobiles from Oshawa or Windsor, insulated cars to keep produce warm, mechanically refrigerated reefers to keep it cold, and tank cars for liquids and chemicals. Flatcars as long as eighty-nine feet carried intermodal containers and semitrailers. Stacking one container atop another had reduced the cost of hauling by 30 per cent, which gave the railway a cost advantage over a cross-country truck.

Whereas sixty cars had once been a big train, now trains of a hundred and thirty cars were seen, carrying two hundred containers and trailers or fifteen hundred automobiles. Permanently coupled "unit trains," which did not have to be broken up and reclassified, carried a single commodity, such as coal, pot-ash or iron ore.

In western Canada, unit trains worked like conveyor belts between coal mines in the foothills of the Rockies, or sulphur and potash deposits in Saskatch-ewan, and terminals on the West Coast and the Great Lakes. Mile-long CN

At Turcot (left), CN's main freight yard in the 1950s, locomotives "flat-switched" cars from track to track. Forty years later, with Turcot converted to intermodal service and renamed Monterm, containers are switched from truck to train by mobile cranes. (Lower photo: Jean B. Héguy)

trains composed of cars supplied by the federal and provincial governments hauled grain from the prairies to the ports.

There had been a time when the railway, with its massive infrastructure of rails, rolling stock, stations, roundhouses, freight sheds and coal depots, had been the most visible industry in the country. Though the train still hauled consumer goods, it no longer delivered to your door or ran through the centre of town. People were therefore less aware of its importance, though five hundred CN freight trains a day snaked through the countryside. One of them covered the world's longest freight run, beginning at Montreal and reaching Vancouver four and a half days, four time zones and 2,900 miles later, with twenty crew changes along the way.

Profit margins were slim, competition fierce. With the railways doing three-quarters of their business west of Winnipeg while losing money in eastern Canada, CN and the CPR began to share rails in areas like the Ottawa Valley and consider merging other services east of Winnipeg.

Though it was carrying two and a half times more freight than a generation earlier, CN's share of the market was barely a quarter of the total freight available, compared with three-quarters in 1950. Moving most of its freight on a third of its tracks, in theory CN could close two-thirds of its operations and affect only 10 per cent of its business. In practice, since those two-thirds provided a feeder system, CN began selling marginal lines to independent operators less constrained by federal regulations and union agreements.

Until 1980 trucks had been the Canadian railways' most worrisome freight competitor. Since then, however, American railways had been deregulated and their lower costs and taxes freed them to offer Canadian shippers cheaper rates for transcontinental traffic. On the other hand, with a quarter of their revenue

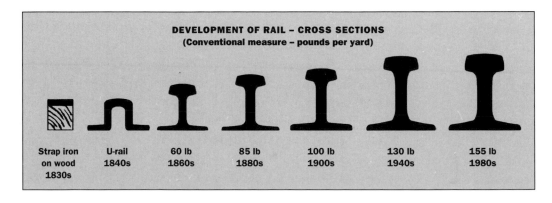

DEVELOPMENT OF RAIL – CROSS SECTIONS
(Conventional measure – pounds per yard)

| Strap iron on wood 1830s | U-rail 1840s | 60 lb 1860s | 85 lb 1880s | 100 lb 1900s | 130 lb 1940s | 155 lb 1980s |

A coal unit train threads through the Fraser Canyon near Lytton en route from Alberta to Vancouver in November 1980. In this slide-prone region the right-of-way is protected by a slide-detector fence.

coming from cross-border freight, CN and the CPR pursued the American market. Though Canadian railways had traditionally trended east-west, in an age of highways, airplanes, television and communications satellites the steel that once bonded the country had lost its political primacy. CN, combining its Grand Trunk Western and other American properties with its Canadian operations under the banner CN North America, extended its U.S. operations south as far as Kentucky and dug the Sarnia Tunnel under the St. Clair River to Port Huron, Michigan, to replace the century-old Grand Trunk tunnel and accommodate double-stack container trains and tri-level automobile carriers.

Although Canada is no longer the "train country" of the past and some have called the railway a sunset industry, the steel wheel on the steel rail remains the most efficient method of moving traffic. It can carry freight with fewer man-hours and a quarter the energy expended by trailer trucks on the highway. A railway right-of-way is easier on the environment and a more economical use of space than an expanding highway system that robs the countryside of precious field and forest. As for passengers, although long-distance services have been steadily eroded for years, there is obvious need for commuter rail transportation around big cities like Montreal and Toronto. Canada's population is too thin and building infrastructure too costly to support the fast intercity supertrains of Japan and Europe – except perhaps someday on the busy routes between Montreal and Toronto or Calgary and Edmonton.

What form railway technology will take in the twenty-first century is open to conjecture. Some foretell a time when there will be only one line from coast to coast. Others suggest that government take over the tracks and charge railways a user fee. Other permutations have been mooted. What is clear, however, is that a technology born of the iron and steam of the Industrial Revolution has a future in the next century.

A BRIEF
CHRONOLOGY

1836   Champlain and St. Lawrence Railroad, Canada's first passenger service.

1849   Railway Guarantee Act launches railway boom.

1852   Grand Trunk Railway incorporated.

1854   Great Western Railway under construction in Ontario.

1856   Grand Trunk Railway completed Quebec City–Toronto.

1857   Great Western builds Canada's first sleeping car.

1864   Grand Trunk assimilates Champlain and St. Lawrence Railroad.

1876   Intercolonial Railway opened.

1879   Federal Department of Railways and Canals created.

1882   Amalgamation of Grand Trunk and Great Western.

1884   Standard Time adopted.

1885   Canadian Pacific Railway reaches Vancouver.

1886   Sod turned for Hudson Bay Railway.

1891   Harvest excursion trains to the prairies become popular.

        St. Clair Tunnel opens at Sarnia.

1896   William Mackenzie and Donald Mann start building Canadian
         Northern Railway.

1897   Crow's Nest Pass Agreement subsidizes grain farmers.

1898   Intercolonial Railway from Moncton reaches Montreal.

1906   Work begins on National Transcontinental Railway.

1907   National Transcontinental's Quebec Bridge collapses, killing
         seventy-five.

1908   Grand Trunk Pacific's first train from Winnipeg to west coast.

1913   Last spike on National Transcontinental.

         Economic depression undermines Canadian Northern and Grand
         Trunk Pacific.

1914-15 Last spike on Grand Trunk Pacific and Canadian Northern.

1915   National Transcontinental joins Canadian Government Railways.

1917   Canadian Northern joins Canadian Government Railways.

1919   Grand Trunk Pacific and Canadian Government Railways join newly
         incorporated Canadian National Railways.

         David Blythe Hanna appointed president.

1922   Sir Henry Thornton appointed chairman and president

1923   CN takes final form with addition of Grand Trunk Railway.

         Thornton moves HQ from Toronto to Montreal.

1923   CN pioneers radio programs to trains.

1925   First CN silk train.

         Diesel-electric car No. 15820 pioneers record-breaking trip Montreal–
         Vancouver.

1927   Central Vermont Railway absorbed by CN.

         Toronto Union Station officially opened.

1928   CN locomotive No. 9000 Canada's first main-line diesel.

1929   First train reaches Churchill, Manitoba.

1930   CN pioneers two-way train phone service.

1932   Thornton resigns; Samuel J. Hungerford becomes acting president.

1934   Trusteeship: Judge C. P. Fullerton, chairman; Hungerford, president.

1936   Co-operation in passenger services between CN and CPR implemented, as required by CN-CPR Act of 1933.

Board of directors replaces trustees; Hungerford, chairman and president.

1939   Royal tour, King George Vl and Queen Elizabeth.

1941   R. C. Vaughan becomes chairman and president.

Centralized Traffic Control (CTC) in Maritimes.

1943   Montreal Central Station opens.

1948   Diesel-electric locomotives introduced into freight service between Montreal and Toronto.

1949   Newfoundland Railway joins CN.

1950   Donald Gordon becomes chairman and president.

1951   Royal tour: Princess Elizabeth covered 3,460 miles on CN lines.

1952   Piggyback freight Montreal–Toronto.

1953   CN Museum Train attracted half a million visitors during tour of twenty-six cities and towns.

1954   CN introduces continuous welded rail into Canada.

1955   *Super Continental* inaugurated Montreal–Toronto–Vancouver.

1960   End of steam: last scheduled CN steam locomotive arrives Winnipeg.

1961   CN's three regions, ten districts and thirty-one divisions reorganized.

New CN symbol designed by Allan Fleming.

CN moves from McGill St. into new HQ over former Canadian Northern Railway Tunnel Station.

1965   Centralized Traffic Control (CTC) extended coast to coast.

        End of CN-CPR passenger pool arrangement in Toronto–Quebec corridor.

        Rapido introduced Montreal–Toronto, offering four-hour, fifty-nine-minute service between Montreal and Toronto, fastest regular passenger run on the continent.

1967   N. J. MacMillan succeeds Donald Gordon as president.

        United Aircraft *Turbo* trains, leased by CN, enter service on Montreal–Toronto run.

1968   Great Slave Lake Railway, 430 miles, completed.

        Buses replace trains in Newfoundland.

1974   R. A. Bandeen named president.

1976   *Turbo* establishes 140-mph speed record.

1976   VIA name and logo introduced as new CN division.

1978   VIA Rail Canada becomes a crown corporation.

1979   CN and CPR telegraph services combine as CNCP.

1981   Ronald E. Lawless named president of CN Rail.

1982   Last run of *Turbo*.

        Maurice LeClair becomes president and CEO.

1985   Lawless named president and CEO of CN.

1988   CN sells hotels and communications.

        Newfoundland Railway closes down.

1989   B. R. D. Smith becomes chairman.

1992   Lawless retires. Paul Tellier becomes president.

INDEX